W9-BJR-333

CONTENTS

Stocking the Pantry, 'Fridge, and Freezer
Equipment and Supplies
Slow Cooker Do's and Don'ts
Slow Cooking Tips

INTRODUCTION

Since the discovery of fire, hungry humans around the globe have slowly cooked less-than-tender morsels of meat and poultry and hard, fibrous vegetables in a simmering pot until the ingredients were tender and tasty. A time-honored technique, this moist heat cooking — cooking in a constantly moving environment of liquid or steam — is now known as braising (from the French word braise, meaning ember).

From the South African potjie, the Persian khoresh, the Moroccan tagine, and the Indian curry to the first American hearth-cooked stew, braised food has been a culinary staple the world over for centuries. But it took Rival Industries' 1960s invention of the Crock-Pot slow cooker to revive and revolutionize slow cooking, which had taken a backseat to baking, broiling, microwaving, and grilling over the years.

The slow cooker is a fairly simple appliance, really. Low-wattage heating coils are sandwiched between inner and outer metal walls, wrapping around the sides and bottom of the slow cooker. A stoneware, metal, or clay insert, which holds the food, fits inside the slow cooker cavity. The coils heat up, the space between the inner and outer walls heats up, and the indirect heat is transferred to the insert, which cooks the ingredients slowly and steadily.

Over time, the Crock-Pot trademark name became a generic reference for all slow cookers. But although all Crock-Pots are slow cookers, all slow cookers are not Crock-Pots. Nearly a dozen companies manufacture slow cookers today, with Hamilton Beach and Crock-Pot dominating the market. (Other manufacturers are: All-Clad, Cuisinart, Kitchen Aid, Presto, Proctor Silex, VitaClay, West Bend, and Williams-Sonoma.)

In developing this book, I set out to revisit global slow cooked culinary classics and convert them for use in the modern-day slow cooker, which has enjoyed a renaissance in the twenty-first century. Today's home cook has never been busier, often juggling a full-time job and a family. The slow cooker is a savior of sorts . . . a family can save money by using less tender cuts of meat and poultry and can save time by loading up the slow cooker, turning it on, and letting the moist heat do what it does best — slowly cooking ingredients to mouthwatering perfection.

I used four different slow cookers to test the recipes I developed for this book: Hamilton Beach Set 'n' Forget, 6-quart cooker with temperature probe and spoon lid (model #33967); Hamilton Beach Premiere Cookware 5½-quart with stovetop searing insert (model #33351); Hamilton Beach 4-Piece Set with 2-quart and 4-quart interchangeable inserts (model #33148); and Proctor Silex 1½-quart with lid latch (model #33116Y).

The two larger slow cookers were great when cooking for six or more or when cooking a roast, ribs, or whole chicken or making soup. The small slow cooker worked wonderfully well for dips, snacks, and desserts. The most versatile, however — and my personal favorite — was the slow cooker with the 2-quart/4-quart interchangeable inserts. The 4-quart was perfect for many recipes serving four to six; the 2-quart worked well for side dishes, servings for two people, and snacks and desserts.

In my extensive testing, I found that the slow cookers all cooked much faster than the manufacturer's stated times for recipe conversions (an observation that friends have noted for other brands of slow cookers as well). I found that in most cases, one hour of conventional cooking equated to about four to five hours in the slow cooker on "low" setting. If meat or poultry cooked for more than six hours, it was likely "falling off the bone" or shredding, both of which are fine for many recipes, like Pulled Pork or Russian Beef Stew but undesirable for Greek Pork Chops or Chicken Dijon.

When it comes to slow cookers, size matters. The cooking insert should be a minimum of one-half to two-thirds full for ingredients to cook in the amount of time stated in a recipe. Filling a slow cooker less than half full will cause the ingredients to cook much faster. The insert should be filled no more than three-quarters full or the simmering ingredients may bubble over the edge of the slow cooker. So it is important that you choose the right size slow cooker when making a recipe. Small slow cookers are available in 1½-, 2-, 2½-, and 3-quart sizes. Medium cookers come in 3½-, 4-, and 4½ quart sizes. Large slow cookers have 5-, 5½-, 6-, and 7-quart capacities. All the appliances are reasonably priced. If your budget allows and you have the storage space, invest in a couple of sizes for maximum versatility.

So get ready, get your passport, and go around the world in your slow cooker — the Middle East for Lebanese Orange-Apricot Chicken; the Caribbean for Bahamian Conch Chowder; India for Rogan Josh; France for Gingered Carrot Vichyssoise; China for Red Cooked Beef; Cuba for Picadillo Stuffed Onions; Southeast Asia for Lamb in Spicy Peanut Sauce; Italy for Neapolitan Genovese; the United Kingdom for Currant-Glazed Corned Beef; and Germany for Shredded Pork and Sauerkraut Sammies. Then head back home to the Americas for some Autumn Harvest Pork Roast, Garlic-Chive Mashed Potatoes, Boston Baked Beans, and Sugar Apple Crisp.

Bon appétit! Buon appetito! Enjoy your meal!

How to use this book

All the recipes in this book are designed to help you create tasty, ethnic-inspired, restaurant quality meals for your family, while you spend your time out of the kitchen on other ventures. Each recipe is accompanied by an easily spotted graphic icon that will alert you to the amount of slow cooking time required, so you'll know how to plan your day:

-4   Less than 4 hours

4–8   4 to 8 hours

8+   8 hours or more

The book is also chock full of helpful tips. Look for the icon at the conclusion of each recipe. You'll find useful information for substitutions, innovations, serving ideas, and ingredient sources.

In the back of the book, look for the detailed pantry, refrigerator, and freezer list, which shows every ingredient you'll need to prepare any recipe in this book as well as necessary kitchen equipment and supplies.

You'll also find must-read Slow Cooker Do's and Don'ts and Slow Cooking Tips that will help you unlock the mysteries of successfully slow cooking the global classic cuisine featured in this book.

Soups and Sauces

Soups

- Gingered Carrot Vichyssoise – *Fusion*
- French Onion Soup – *France*
- Chorizo and Split Pea Soup – *Spain/Portugal*
- Ham and Navy Bean Soup – *USA*
- Pasta e Fagioli – *Italy*
- "Puy" Lentil Soup – *France*
- Bahamian Conch Chowder – *Caribbean*
- Cioppino – *Italy*
- Rhode Island Clam Chowder – *USA*
- Mulligatawny Soup – *India*
- Lamb and Herb Couscous Soup – *Middle East*
- Chunky Two-Meat Chili – *USA*
- Chuckwagon Cowboy Chili – *USA*
- Wicked Chicken Sausage White Chili – *USA*

Sauces

- Neapolitan Meat Ragù – *Italy*
- Veal and Mushroom Bolognese Sauce – *Italy*
- Chardonnay Pumpkin Sausage Sauce – *Italy*
- Mushroom, Tomato, and Artichoke Sauce – *USA*
- Real Deal Italian Meatless Sauce – *Italy*
- Sausage Puttanesca Sauce – *Italy*
- Peach Chutney – *India*
- Pink Banana Butter – *Caribbean*

Gingered Carrot Vichyssoise

 8+

Whereas the Irish may lay claim to hearty potato soup, the origin of vichyssoise — potato and leek soup served cold — is hotly debated between France and America. This version, however, is a fusion of many cultures. The addition of carrots, orange juice, and gingerroot to the vichyssoise provides a subtle Asian influence.

1 tablespoon olive oil

1 teaspoon garlic paste or finely minced garlic

1½ tablespoons gingerroot paste or finely minced gingerroot

1 leek, white part only, halved, washed well, and thinly sliced

8 large carrots, peeled and sliced into 1-inch-thick pieces

2 large Yukon Gold potatoes, peeled, halved lengthwise, and cut into 1-inch-thick pieces

2 bay leaves

½ cup orange juice

1 (32-ounce) carton College Inn White Wine & Herb Culinary Broth

2½ cups chicken broth

1 teaspoon salt

½ teaspoon black pepper

1 cup heavy cream

Snipped fresh chives

Place oil in a large nonstick skillet over medium-low heat. Add garlic, gingerroot, and leeks, and sauté for 3 minutes, until leeks are soft. Transfer to a 4-quart slow cooker. Add carrots, potatoes, bay leaves, orange juice, broths, salt, and pepper. Stir to combine. Cover slow cooker and cook on low setting for 8 to 9 hours, until carrots and potatoes are soft.

Remove bay leaves. Place soup in a blender and puree in batches. Transfer to a large covered container. Stir in cream, cover, and refrigerate until needed.

To serve: Stir soup and ladle it into large, shallow soup bowls. Sprinkle each serving with chives.

You can serve this soup chilled or warm. To reheat, place soup in a large nonstick saucepan over low heat until it is heated through. (Do not allow soup to come to a boil.)

Makes: 12 cups

French Onion Soup

 8+

The secret to a great French onion soup is in the broth, not in the thick crusty bread or oozing cheese topping so often found in restaurants. In this recipe the sweet flavor of slowly cooked caramelized onions shines through a delicately seasoned broth. The Gruyère croutes hide under cover, soaking up the flavors of the soup and offering a hidden cheesy bonus.

6 large sweet onions, like Vidalia, peeled, cut in half, and thinly sliced

½ cup butter, melted

1 teaspoon sugar

½ cup dry sherry

4 cups beef broth

2 cups chicken broth

1 teaspoon snipped fresh thyme or ⅓ teaspoon dried

1 teaspoon snipped fresh flat-leaf parsley or ⅓ teaspoon dried

½ teaspoon salt

¼ teaspoon black pepper

1 small (9-ounce) baguette, cut into 1-inch slices (about 16 slices)

2 cloves garlic, peeled and cut in half

1 tablespoon Dijon mustard

1½ cups shredded Gruyère or Swiss cheese

Place onions in a 6-quart slow cooker. Pour melted butter over onions. Cover and cook on low setting for 9½ to 10 hours, until onions have caramelized.

Place sugar in a large bowl. Add sherry and whisk until sugar is dissolved. Add beef and chicken broths, thyme, parsley, salt, and pepper. Whisk until well combined. Pour broth mixture into slow cooker. Stir to mix well with onions. Cook on low setting for 2 hours.

While soup is cooking, make the Gruyère croutes: Preheat oven to 300°F. Place baguette slices on a nonstick baking sheet. Bake for 15 minutes. Remove from oven. Rub cut side of each half-clove of garlic over the top of 4 baguette slices. Spread a thin layer of mustard over each baguette slice. Top each slice with an equal amount of cheese, packing into a tight mound. Bake croutes for 5 minutes or until cheese has melted.

To serve: Place 1½ cups onion soup in each bowl. Tuck 2 Gruyère croutes into the soup in each bowl so that only the cheesy tops are exposed. Serve immediately.

The raw onions will fill the slow cooker to the brim, but don't worry; they cook down to a quarter of the volume as they caramelize. You can transfer cooked soup to a covered container and refrigerate or freeze until needed. (Don't add the croutes until you gently reheat the soup in a large saucepan over low heat.) You can make croutes several hours ahead and store them at room temperature in a zipper bag. The hot soup will melt the cheese again.

Serves: 8

Chorizo and Split Pea Soup

 8+

Chorizo is fermented, cured pork sausage originating in Spain and Portugal on the Iberian Peninsula. In the United States, you are more likely to find Mexican chorizo sausage, which is offered uncooked or smoked. Whether you use Spanish, Portuguese, or Mexican chorizo, be sure it is the cured, smoked variety.

1 tablespoon olive oil

8 ounces slim chorizo sticks, casings removed and thinly sliced

1 cup chopped sweet onions, like Vidalia

½ cup minced celery

½ cup minced carrots

1½ teaspoons garlic paste or minced garlic

8 to 10 ounces green split peas, rinsed and picked over

1 (32-ounce) carton chicken broth

2 cups water

½ teaspoon dried thyme

Salt and pepper

Croutons or oyster crackers

Place olive oil in a large nonstick skillet over medium heat. Add chorizo, onions, celery, carrots, garlic, and split peas. Sauté for 3 minutes, stirring frequently. Transfer to a 4-quart slow cooker. Add chicken broth, water, and thyme. Stir to mix well. Cover and cook on low setting for 8 to 10 hours, until split peas are tender. Season soup with salt and pepper to taste.

Puree soup in batches in a blender. Return soup to slow cooker and hold on warm until ready to serve, up to 1 hour. Sprinkle each serving with croutons or oyster crackers.

To use uncooked chorizo, remove casings and cook sausage in a nonstick skillet over medium heat, breaking it into small pieces. Drain sausage on paper toweling before adding to slow cooker.

Serves: 6

Ham and Navy Bean Soup

 4–8

Every year at the first sign of autumn, family, friends, and co-workers beg cosmetologist Dana Munn for her ham and navy bean soup. She usually makes up two slow cookers full of this tasty, comforting soup and shares it with everyone, even clients like me!

1 (1-pound) package dried navy beans

1 tablespoon olive oil

½ pound ham, finely chopped

½ cup finely chopped sweet onions, like Vidalia

½ cup finely chopped peeled carrots

½ cup finely chopped celery

1 bunch fresh kale, washed, spun dry, and finely chopped

2 teaspoons garlic paste or finely minced garlic

1 (14.5-ounce) can chicken broth

½ teaspoon crushed red pepper flakes

1 teaspoon hot sauce

1 bay leaf

½ teaspoon white pepper

1 packet Goya or Badia sazón (coriander and annatto seasoning, see below)

Sort through beans, discarding broken ones. Place beans in a large nonstick saucepan over medium-high heat. Add water to cover beans by 2 inches. Bring to a boil, stir beans, then turn off burner. Allow beans to soften in saucepan until most of the water has been absorbed, about 1 hour. Drain beans in a colander. Rinse beans and drain again. Transfer beans to a 5- or 6-quart slow cooker.

Meanwhile, place oil in a large nonstick skillet over medium heat. When oil is hot, add ham, onions, carrots, celery, kale, and garlic. Sauté, stirring frequently, until vegetables are tender, about 4 minutes. Transfer vegetables to slow cooker. Add chicken broth, red pepper flakes, hot sauce, bay leaf, white pepper, and Goya seasoning to slow cooker. Stir to combine ingredients. Add water so that slow cooker is three-quarters full.

Stir ingredients, cover slow cooker, and cook on low setting for 6 to 8 hours. Remove bay leaf before serving.

Both Goya and Badia brands make a sazón (seasoning) blend of coriander, annatto, salt, garlic, dehydrated onion, paprika, and other Spanish spices. It usually can be found in the Spanish section of your supermarket or at a Spanish grocery, or find it at www.badia-spices.com or www.goya.com. Look for ends of spiral-cut ham at your local deli or supermarket meat section. They are meaty and inexpensive.

Serves: 8 to 10

Pasta e Fagioli

 8+

One of Italy's most beloved soups, this bean and pasta soup is a hearty meal in itself, and great on a chilly autumn or winter night. Serve with fresh Italian bread and a salad of fruit or leafy greens.

8 ounces (about 1¼ cups) dried Great Northern beans

¼ pound salt pork, finely diced

2 cups chopped sweet onions, like Vidalia

1 (14.5-ounce) can petite-cut tomatoes with garlic and olive oil

2 teaspoons garlic paste or finely minced garlic

2 teaspoons instant beef bouillon granules

5 cups water

½ teaspoon coarse/kosher salt

¼ teaspoon cracked black pepper

1 cup pipette pasta or miniature shells, bows, or elbow macaroni

One day ahead: Place dried beans in a large bowl. Add water to cover beans by 3 inches. Allow beans to soak at room temperature overnight.

Early in the day: Drain beans in a colander. Rinse and drain again. Place beans in a 4-quart slow cooker.

Place salt pork in a large nonstick skillet over medium heat. Cook pork, stirring constantly for 2 minutes. Remove pork with a slotted spoon and drain on paper toweling. Add pork to slow cooker. Add onions to skillet and sauté until translucent, about 3 minutes. Transfer onions to slow cooker.

Drain tomatoes in a sieve, reserving juices (about ½ cup). Add tomatoes to slow cooker. Whisk garlic into reserved tomato juice and add to slow cooker.

Dissolve beef bouillon granules in 5 cups water. Add to slow cooker. Add salt and pepper and stir until all ingredients are well combined.

Cover slow cooker and cook on low setting for 8 hours, until beans are al dente. Add pasta to slow cooker and cook 30 to 45 minutes more, until pasta is al dente and beans are tender.

Pipette pasta looks like a cross between elbow macaroni and miniature shells. You can substitute bacon for the salt pork if desired.

Serves: 6

"Puy" Lentil Soup

 8+

Peppery French green lentils are the most delicate type of lentils. Originally grown in the Puy region of France, the lentils are actually small, dark, and speckled. They hold their shape well without becoming mushy, but they must cook longer than other types of lentils.

1 pound French green lentils, rinsed and picked over

1 ham bone

1 cup chopped baby carrots

1 cup chopped sweet onions, like Vidalia

1 cup chopped celery

3 tablespoons minced curly parsley

1 teaspoon garlic paste or finely minced garlic

8 cups water

2 (14.5-ounce) cans petite-cut diced tomatoes with garlic and olive oil, with juices

2 tablespoons sugar

½ teaspoon dried oregano

½ teaspoon salt

¼ teaspoon black pepper

2 tablespoons white wine vinegar

2 cups small croutons

Place lentils, ham bone, carrots, onions, celery, and parsley in a 6-quart slow cooker. Whisk garlic paste into 1 cup water. Add to slow cooker. Pour remaining 7 cups water into slow cooker. Stir to mix ingredients well. Cover and cook on low setting for 4 hours.

Mix tomatoes, sugar, oregano, salt, pepper, and vinegar together in a medium bowl. Add to slow cooker. Stir to combine. Cover and cook on low setting for 5 hours more, until lentils and vegetables are tender.

Remove ham bone. Cut off any tender pieces of ham. Cut into bite-size pieces and add to soup. Sprinkle croutons over each serving.

You can transfer soup to a covered container and refrigerate or freeze until needed. Reheat soup in a nonstick saucepan over low heat.

Serves: 8

Bahamian Conch Chowder

 4–8

A true Bahamian soup, this conch chowder resembles the eighteenth-century island original, long-simmered in a classic tomato base. Early Bahamians believed consuming conch would enhance male potency, a long-held mysticism that may explain why the soup recipe made its way with island immigrants who settled in the Florida Keys.

1 teaspoon olive oil

2½ cups chopped sweet onions, like Vidalia

1½ cups chopped green bell peppers

2 teaspoons garlic paste or finely minced garlic

2 (14.5-ounce) cans petite-diced tomatoes with juices

1 (6-ounce) can tomato paste

1½ cups water

1 teaspoon dried marjoram

½ teaspoon dried sage

¼ teaspoon dried thyme

1 teaspoon dried parsley

½ teaspoon dried oregano

¾ teaspoon salt

¼ teaspoon cracked pepper

¼ teaspoon cayenne pepper

1 tablespoon barbecue sauce

1 pound tenderized fresh conch, cut into ¼-inch dice, or 1 pound ground conch

1 cup diced ham

1 ham bone

Cream sherry or Busha Browne's Spicy & Hot Pepper Sherry sauce (optional)

Place oil in a large nonstick skillet over medium heat. When oil is hot, add onions, bell peppers, and garlic. Sauté, stirring frequently, until onions are soft, about 5 minutes. Place onion mixture in a 4-quart slow cooker.

Add tomatoes, tomato paste, water, marjoram, sage, thyme, parsley, oregano, salt, cracked and cayenne peppers, barbecue sauce, conch, and diced ham to slow cooker. Stir until ingredients are well combined. Place ham bone in slow cooker, pushing it down to the bottom of the cooker. Cover slow cooker and cook on low setting for 5 to 6 hours, or until conch is tender.

To serve: Remove ham bone and discard. Transfer chowder to individual soup bowls. Lace each serving with cream sherry or hot pepper sherry sauce if desired.

Unless it is put through a tenderizing machine or pounded for many laborious minutes, conch is very tough. Conch can no longer be taken from U.S. waters, so it is most often imported from the Bahamas. If you don't live in Florida or the Keys, where conch is usually sold in local fish markets, you can order it online from: www.keysfisheries.com.

Serves: 10 to 12

Cioppino

A consummate fisherman and a great cook, my friend Bill Hendrick has put together this exquisite Italian fish stew that even a landlubber can easily create with a simple stop at the supermarket fish counter.

1 tablespoon olive oil
1 cup chopped sweet onions, like Vidalia
6 teaspoons garlic paste or finely minced garlic
2 (14.5-ounce) cans diced tomatoes with basil, oregano, and garlic, plus juices
3 (14.5-ounce) cans chicken broth
Dash hot sauce
1 cup full-bodied red wine, like Shiraz or Zinfandel
¼ cup snipped fresh basil
3 bay leaves
1 pound large shrimp (16/20s), peeled and deveined
1 (8-ounce) can fresh lump crabmeat
½ to ¾ pound bay scallops
½ to 1 pound firm white fish fillets, such as halibut, snapper, or grouper, cut in bite-size pieces
Salt and freshly ground black pepper
Freshly grated Parmesan cheese
¼ cup snipped fresh parsley

Place oil in a large nonstick skillet over medium heat. Add onions and sauté until softened, stirring frequently, for about 2 minutes. Add garlic and sauté, stirring constantly, for 1 minute.

Transfer onion mixture to a 5-quart slow cooker. Add tomatoes, broth, hot sauce, wine, basil, and bay leaves. Stir to combine. Cover and cook on low heat for 6 to 8 hours, until the broth is rich and hot.

Add shrimp, crabmeat, bay scallops, and fish. Cover slow cooker and cook on high setting for 20 minutes or until shrimp turn pink and fish and scallops turn opaque. (Do not overcook.) Remove bay leaves. Season with salt and pepper to taste.

To serve: Serve cioppino in large, shallow soup bowls. Sprinkle each serving with Parmesan cheese and parsley.

Serve with hot, crusty artisan bread for dipping in the flavorful broth.

Serves: 4 to 6

Rhode Island Clam Chowder

 4–8

Most folks have tasted creamy New England clam chowder and probably have at least heard of the tomato-red Manhattan version. But unless you have lived or vacationed in Rhode Island, chances are you have yet to discover the tasty clear-broth chowder so cherished in the tiny state. The essential ingredient for authentic Rhode Island chowder is quahogs, large hard-shelled clams with a distinctively briny taste. Quahogs are tough, so they must be chopped and cooked for a long period of time. Since fresh chopped quahogs are difficult to find if you're not on the Atlantic seacoast, I've substituted frozen or canned chopped clams and whole baby clams. (See 🕐 *below.)*

6 slices bacon, cut into ½-inch pieces

1½ cups chopped sweet onions, like Vidalia

3 cups peeled, diced (½-inch) Yukon Gold potatoes (about 3 large)

3 (8-ounce) bottles clam juice

3 cups chicken broth

3 tablespoons snipped fresh dill

2 teaspoons black pepper

1 teaspoon salt

Pinch cayenne pepper

1 pound flash-frozen clam meat or 3 (6-ounce) cans chopped clams
  plus 1 (10-ounce) can whole baby clams, drained

Fry bacon in a large nonstick skillet over medium heat until crispy. Remove with a slotted spoon and drain on paper toweling. Discard all but 1 tablespoon bacon grease. Add onions and sauté until browned, about 5 minutes. Transfer onions and bacon to a 4-quart slow cooker. Add potatoes, clam juice, broth, dill, pepper, salt, and cayenne. Stir to combine.

Cover slow cooker and cook on low setting for 6 hours. Stir in clams. Re-cover slow cooker and cook on low setting for 30 minutes more. Serve immediately or keep on warm setting for up to 1 hour.

🕐 If you do have access to fresh quahogs, use 1 quart chopped clams with juices reserved. (You can substitute the juices for some of the bottled clam juice.) Add the chopped quahogs after 4 hours of cooking the broth and cook for 2½ hours more.

Makes: 10 cups

Mulligatawny Soup

 4–8

Originating in southern India, mulligatawny (or pepper water) soup found its way to England and South Africa, thanks to the British military and diplomats who served in the colonial services in the Madras region in the late eighteenth century.

4 pounds cut-up chicken pieces, skin removed

Salt and black pepper

1 teaspoon curry powder

⅛ teaspoon ground cloves

⅛ teaspoon ground allspice

⅛ teaspoon cayenne pepper

1 teaspoon gingerroot paste or finely minced gingerroot

1 teaspoon garlic paste or finely minced garlic

4 cups water

2 tablespoons butter

2 cups sliced and quartered sweet onions, like Vidalia

2 tablespoons flour

⅓ cup golden raisins

1 apple, peeled, cored, and cut into ½-inch pieces

1 green or red bell pepper, cut into ½-inch dice (about 1 cup)

1 cup peeled, chopped tomatoes

1 teaspoon lemon juice

Grated Parmesan cheese

Snipped fresh parsley

Place chicken in a 4-quart slow cooker. Season with 1½ teaspoons salt, curry powder, cloves, allspice, and cayenne pepper. Whisk gingerroot and garlic pastes into 4 cups water. Pour water over chicken. (If you are using minced gingerroot and garlic, sprinkle them over chicken and then pour water into slow cooker.) Cover slow cooker and cook on low setting until chicken is tender, 4 to 4½ hours.

Remove chicken from slow cooker and place on a plate to cool. Pour chicken broth through a fine-meshed strainer into a large bowl. Measure broth. Add water to make 6 cups. Pour broth into slow cooker. Cover and set temperature to warm.

Melt butter in a large nonstick skillet over medium heat. Add onions and sauté, stirring frequently, for 4 minutes or until onions are soft. Stir flour into onions. Remove 1 cup warm broth from slow cooker and gradually pour it into skillet, stirring constantly. Transfer onion mixture to slow cooker and re-cover.

With clean hands, remove cooked chicken from bones, discarding any remaining skin or gristle. Chop chicken into bite-size pieces. Add chicken, raisins, apples, bell peppers, and tomatoes to slow cooker. Cover slow cooker and cook for 2 to 2½ hours, until flavors marry. Add lemon juice and season soup with salt and pepper to taste (about ¾ teaspoon salt and ½ teaspoon pepper).

To serve: Serve soup in large shallow bowls, sprinkled with Parmesan cheese and parsley.

Variations include adding chopped carrots or turnips. Authentically the soup is served with a side of plain or spiced rice.

Serves: 8

Lamb and Herb Couscous Soup

🕐 4–8

Pearl couscous are small, round, white, pasta-like granules made from semolina and wheat flour. Unlike the small, yellow, North African couscous, pearl couscous (also called Israeli couscous) are toasted rather than dried, have a chewy bite, and can hold their own in a brothy soup. Barley-shaped egg noodles, such as Manischewitz brand, make a good substitute.

4 pieces bacon, thinly sliced

1 pound lamb, cut into bite-size pieces

2 cups chopped sweet onions, like Vidalia

2 tablespoons flour

4 cups beef broth

3 cups College Inn White Wine & Herb Culinary Broth

1 cup chopped roasted red peppers (from a jar)

¼ cup tomato paste

1 teaspoon Hungarian paprika

1 teaspoon whole fennel seeds

½ teaspoon coarse black pepper

1 teaspoon coarse salt

2 tablespoons snipped fresh cilantro

1 cup pearl couscous

½ cup sweet orange marmalade

Cook bacon in a large nonstick skillet over medium heat until crispy. Remove bacon from skillet with a slotted spoon and drain it on paper toweling. Add lamb to skillet and cook until browned, about 2 minutes. Remove lamb from skillet with a slotted spoon and drain it on paper toweling. Transfer bacon and lamb to a 5-quart slow cooker.

Add onions to skillet and sauté until softened, about 2 minutes. Stir in flour. Slowly stir in beef broth, stirring constantly until smooth. Transfer onions and broth to slow cooker.

Add culinary broth, roasted peppers, tomato paste, paprika, fennel seeds, pepper, salt, and cilantro to slow cooker. Stir to combine ingredients. Cover slow cooker and cook on low setting for 6 to 7 hours, until lamb is tender. Add couscous and marmalade and stir ingredients. Re-cover slow cooker and cook for 30 minutes more.

🕐 Look for inexpensive, shoulder cuts of lamb for this recipe. Trim off all the fat and bone and cut meat into bite-size pieces. You can find Israeli couscous at www.riceriverfarms.com. I use mildly hot Hungarian paprika in this recipe. (You can buy paprika ranging from sweet to hot.) You can order the spicy paprika at www.penzeys.com or substitute regular supermarket paprika if you don't want the peppery kick.

Makes: 10 cups

Chunky Two-Meat Chili

 4–8

My friend Suzanne Tobey found this great chili while tasting scores of creations at her grandson's California elementary school chili cook-off.

1 pound boneless beef chuck roast, excess fat removed, cut into ¾-inch pieces
1 pound pork tenderloin, cut into ¾-inch pieces
¼ cup flour
1 tablespoon olive oil
2 (10-ounce) cans diced tomatoes and green chiles, with juices
1 (16 ounce) can pinto beans, with juices
1 (12-ounce) can beer
½ cup chopped sweet onions, like Vidalia
2 tablespoons chili powder
1 teaspoon ground cumin
½ teaspoon garlic powder
1 teaspoon salt, divided
⅛ teaspoon ground cinnamon
½ cup shredded cheddar cheese

Place beef and pork pieces in a large bowl. Sprinkle flour over meat and toss with a large spoon until meat is well coated with flour. Place oil in a large nonstick skillet over medium heat. When oil is hot, add meat and sauté, stirring constantly, until meat is browned. Transfer meat to a 4- or 5-quart slow cooker with a slotted spoon.

Add tomatoes, pinto beans, beer, onions, chili powder, cumin, garlic powder, ½ teaspoon salt, and cinnamon to slow cooker. Stir to combine ingredients.

Cover slow cooker and cook on low setting for 6 to 7 hours, until beef and pork are fork-tender.

To serve: Adjust seasoning with ½ teaspoon salt (optional) before serving. Top each portion of chili with shredded cheddar cheese

Beer enhances the flavor of the chili as well as acting as a meat tenderizer. Serve with cornbread and honey butter.

Makes: 8 cups

Chuckwagon Cowboy Chili

 4–8

My nephew Matthew Shearer, a chef in Portland, Oregon, created this hearty chili especially for this book. The interesting combination of ingredients and seasonings makes this a restaurant-quality dish. Matt recommends a variety of toppings for this chili: shredded cheddar or pepper jack cheese, minced onions, diced tomatoes, or diced avocadoes.

2 tablespoons olive oil, divided

2 cups chopped sweet onions, like Vidalia

1 red bell pepper, chopped

1 green bell pepper, chopped

4 teaspoons garlic paste or finely minced garlic

1 pound ground grass-fed chuck

1 pound ground bison

1½ pounds grass-fed chuck roast, excess fat removed and cut into ¾-inch pieces

1 (14-ounce) can petite diced tomatoes, with juices

2 cups beef broth

1 (11.5-ounce) can V-8 juice

1 (6-ounce) can tomato paste with basil, garlic, and oregano

1 (4-ounce) can mild green chilies

3 tablespoons chili powder

2 tablespoons ground cumin

1 tablespoon onion powder

2 tablespoons Worcestershire sauce

3 tablespoons soy sauce

¼ cup minced jalapeño peppers with seeds (about 3)

Place 1 tablespoon olive oil in a large nonstick skillet over medium heat. Add onions, chopped bell peppers, and garlic. Sauté, stirring frequently, for 2 minutes, until onions are translucent. Add ground chuck and ground bison, and sauté until meat has browned, about 5 minutes. Transfer meat and vegetables to a 5-quart slow cooker with a slotted spoon.

Discard meat juices and wipe out skillet with paper toweling. Add remaining 1 tablespoon oil to skillet. Add beef pieces and sauté until browned, about 2 minutes. Transfer to slow cooker with slotted spoon.

Add tomatoes, broth, V-8 juice, tomato paste, green chilies, chili powder, cumin, onion powder, Worcestershire sauce, soy sauce, and minced jalapeños to slow cooker. Stir to mix ingredients.

Cook chili on low setting for 6 to 7 hours.

Bison and grass-fed beef make this chili more like the type served on the chuckwagons out on the range in the Wild West. You can substitute regular corn-fed beef if you'd like.

Makes: 14 cups

Wicked Chicken Sausage White Chili

 4–8

Wickedly spicy, wickedly tasty, this brothy chili is unlike its tomato-based cousins. The secret lies within the special chicken sausages.

½ pound Mozzarella and Roasted Garlic Chicken Sausage (see 🕐 below)
1 tablespoon olive oil
2 cups chopped sweet onions, like Vidalia
1¾ pounds boneless, skinless chicken breasts, cut into ½-inch dice
1 (15.8-ounce) can Great Northern beans, rinsed and drained
1½ cups frozen gold-and-white corn
3 cups chicken broth
1 teaspoon ground cumin
1 teaspoon dried oregano leaves
⅛ teaspoon cayenne pepper
¼ teaspoon salt
1 burrito-size flour tortilla
2 teaspoons fresh lime juice

Cut casings off sausages, then chop sausages into ½-inch dice. Set aside. Place oil in a large nonstick skillet over medium heat. Add onions and sauté for 2 minutes, stirring frequently, until soft. Add chicken and sauté for 2 minutes, stirring frequently, until browned. Add sausage and sauté for 1 minute, stirring constantly. Transfer mixture to a 5-quart slow cooker.

Stir in beans, corn, broth, cumin, oregano, cayenne, and salt. Cook on low setting for 4 hours.

Meanwhile, make lime tortilla strips. Preheat oven to 350°F. Coat tortilla with olive oil spray. Sprinkle with lime juice. Cut tortilla into thin strips with a pizza cutter. Place strips on a nonstick baking sheet. Bake for 5 minutes. Turn strips with a firm spatula and bake 5 minutes more. Allow strips to cool. Store them in a freezer-weight zipper bag at room temperature until needed.

To serve: Serve chili sprinkled with lime tortilla strips.

🕐You can find the spicy chicken sausage at Sam's Club. It is made with smoked mozzarella cheese, roasted garlic, artichokes, and an array of spices that give the chili a special kick. If you can't find this sausage, substitute another spicy chicken sausage.

Serves: 8

Neapolitan Meat Ragù

 8+

In Italy, this meat-flavored sauce (ragù) traditionally is served on pasta as a first course. The meat itself is removed from the sauce and served as a separate course. You can, instead, cut the meat and sausage into bite-size pieces or thin slices and serve them atop sauced pasta immediately. Because this recipe easily can be made ahead and refrigerated or frozen, I've written the directions accordingly.

½ tablespoon olive oil

6 ounces lean steak, such as sirloin or tenderloin, cut into 2-inch chunks

8 ounces boneless pork, such as a boneless chop or portion of loin roast, cut into 2-inch chunks

1 (12-ounce) package Roasted Garlic and Gruyère Cheese Turkey Sausage links, cut in half

1 cup chopped sweet onions, like Vidalia

½ cup good red drinking wine

2 (35-ounce) cans peeled plum tomatoes with juices, like San Marzano brand

2 teaspoons Gourmet Garden Mediterranean Herb and Spice Blend paste

Kosher or coarse salt

¼ teaspoon crushed red pepper flakes

Place oil in a large nonstick skillet over medium heat. When oil is hot, add steak and pork and brown all sides, about 2 minutes. Transfer meat to a 4-quart slow cooker with a slotted spoon. Add turkey sausage to slow cooker.

Sauté onions in skillet for 2 minutes, stirring frequently and scraping up any meat bits. Add wine and cook, stirring occasionally, until wine has evaporated, about 3 minutes. Transfer onions to slow cooker.

Puree tomatoes and juices in a blender, then add to slow cooker. Add seasoning blend paste, 2 teaspoons salt, and red pepper flakes. Stir to combine ingredients.

Cover slow cooker and cook on low setting for 8 hours, stirring after 4 hours. Remove meat from sauce, place in a covered container, and refrigerate until needed. Season sauce with 1 teaspoon salt or to taste. Transfer sauce to covered containers and refrigerate or freeze until needed.

It is important to use lean meats and precooked turkey sausage (any flavor is fine) in this recipe so that excess fat is not rendered during the long simmering process.

Makes: 9 cups sauce

Veal and Mushroom Bolognese Sauce

 8+

Whereas Spaghetti alla Bolognese is a popular Italian dish around the globe, in Bologna itself, the meaty sauce would never be served with spaghetti — a durum wheat pasta found nearer to Naples. True Bolognese sauce traditionally would be served with an egg noodle, like tagliatelle.

½ ounce (about ½ cup) dried mushrooms, like chanterelles
¼ cup finely diced bacon
1 teaspoon garlic paste or finely minced garlic
1 cup chopped onions, like Vidalia
1 cup finely chopped celery
⅓ cup finely chopped baby carrots
1 pound ground veal
1 (8-ounce) can tomato sauce with basil, garlic, and oregano
1 (14.5-ounce) can diced tomatoes with basil, garlic, and oregano, with juices
½ cup dry red wine
¾ teaspoon salt
¼ teaspoon ground allspice
⅛ teaspoon black pepper

Place mushrooms in a medium bowl. Pour 1 cup warm water over mushrooms and allow them to soak for 30 minutes.

Meanwhile, place bacon in a large nonstick skillet over medium heat. Cook bacon for 1 minute, stirring constantly. Add garlic, onions, celery, and carrots to skillet. Sauté for 2 minutes, stirring frequently. Add veal and sauté, stirring frequently, until meat is browned, about 3 minutes.

Transfer veal mixture to a 4-quart slow cooker. Add tomato sauce, diced tomatoes with juices, wine, salt, allspice, and pepper to slow cooker. Stir until ingredients are well combined.

Drain mushrooms in a medium sieve. Rinse mushrooms and drain again. Add mushrooms to slow cooker and stir to combine. Cook on low setting for 8 hours. Serve immediately atop pasta of your choice or transfer to a covered container and refrigerate or freeze until needed.

You can substitute any kind of dried mushrooms for the chanterelles.

Makes: 6 cups

Chardonnay Pumpkin Sausage Sauce -4

Perfect for Halloween night supper over a steaming plate of penne pasta, this pumpkin sauce is smooth, rich, and flavorful. To make the most of pumpkin season, clean and cook fresh pumpkin much as you would a butternut squash — baked and scooped from shell or peeled and boiled or steamed.

1 pound pork sausage, like Jimmy Dean

¼ teaspoon crushed red pepper flakes

1 cup chopped sweet onions, like Vidalia

10 cloves garlic, thinly sliced

1 tablespoon snipped fresh sage or 1 teaspoon dried sage leaves

1 (15-ounce) can pumpkin puree (or 1½ to 2 cups cooked pureed pumpkin)

½ cup chardonnay wine

1½ cups College Inn White Wine & Herb Culinary Broth

½ teaspoon salt

⅛ teaspoon ground cinnamon

1 tablespoon sugar

Place sausage and red pepper flakes in a large nonstick skillet over medium heat. Cook sausage for 2 minutes, breaking it into small pieces with a wooden spoon. Add onions and garlic and sauté, stirring frequently, for 2 more minutes. Transfer sausage mixture to a 4-quart slow cooker.

Add pumpkin puree, wine, broth, salt, cinnamon, and sugar to slow cooker. Stir until all ingredients are well combined and smooth. Cover slow cooker and cook on low setting for 3½ hours. Serve over pasta or transfer to covered containers and refrigerate or freeze until needed.

Substitute spicy sausage or a specialty sausage in this recipe if you like. The College Inn broth is actually chicken broth spiked with wine and herbs. You can use regular chicken broth in this recipe without significantly changing the flavor of the sauce.

Makes: 8 cups

Mushroom, Tomato, and Artichoke Sauce 4–8

This hearty meatless sauce is great tossed with cheese tortellini or tubular pasta, such as penne. It also makes a tasty Italian-style topping for grilled chicken or fish. For a super-easy soup, simmer together 4 cups Chardonnay Pumpkin Sausage Sauce (recipe, preceding page), 2 cups Mushroom, Tomato, and Artichoke Sauce, and 4 cups College Inn White Wine & Culinary Broth. Yummy!

1 tablespoon olive oil

1 cup chopped sweet onions, like Vidalia

2 teaspoons garlic paste or finely minced garlic

2 (10-ounce) packages fresh button mushrooms, wiped clean and sliced (about 7 cups)

2 (14-ounce) cans artichoke hearts, drained and chopped

2 tablespoons capers, rinsed and drained

1 (2.25-ounce) can sliced ripe olives, drained

2 (14.5-ounce) cans Hunt's Diced Fire-roasted Tomatoes with Garlic, with juices

1 (8-ounce) can tomato sauce with basil, garlic, and oregano

¼ cup white wine

Place oil in a large nonstick skillet over medium heat. Add onions and garlic and sauté, stirring constantly, for 1 minute. Add mushrooms and sauté, stirring frequently, for 4 minutes. Transfer mushroom mixture to a 4-quart slow cooker.

Add chopped artichokes, capers, olives, diced tomatoes with juices, tomato sauce, and wine. Stir to combine ingredients. Cover slow cooker and cook on low setting for 4 hours.

Transfer 3 cups sauce to a blender. Puree until smooth. Return puree to slow cooker and stir into sauce. Serve immediately atop pasta of your choice or transfer to covered containers and refrigerate or freeze until needed.

You can substitute more exotic mushrooms for the white button variety if your budget allows.

Makes: 8 cups

Real Deal Italian Meatless Sauce

 8+

When tomato sauce packed with flavorful vegetables, herbs, and spices simmers all day — that's Italian. Commonly referred to as gravy by Italian cooks in the old country, the sauce traditionally is made in large quantities and is used with all kinds of pasta as well as becoming the base for a myriad of dishes. Use this sauce when making Braciole (page 54) and Chicken and Sausage Manicotti (page 104).

1 cup dried porcini mushrooms

1 tablespoon olive oil

2 cups chopped sweet onions, like Vidalia

1 cup finely chopped celery

2 teaspoons garlic paste or finely minced garlic

1 cup snipped fresh flat-leaf parsley

1 teaspoon snipped fresh rosemary

½ teaspoon dried sage leaves

1 (28-ounce) can San Marzano whole tomatoes or other canned Roma tomatoes, with juices

1 (14.5-ounce) can Hunt's Diced Fire Roasted Tomatoes with Garlic, juices reserved

4 (8-ounce) cans tomato sauce with basil, garlic, and oregano

1 small dried red chile pepper

1½ teaspoons salt

Place dried mushrooms in a small bowl. Add water until mushrooms are just covered. Set aside.

Meanwhile, place oil in a large nonstick skillet over medium heat. Add onions, celery, garlic, parsley, rosemary, and sage. Sauté for 5 minutes, stirring frequently. Transfer vegetables to a 4-quart slow cooker. Remove whole tomatoes from juices with a slotted spoon and coarsely chop them. Add chopped and diced tomatoes, juices, tomato sauce, chile pepper, and salt to slow cooker. Stir to combine ingredients.

Remove mushrooms from soaking liquid with a slotted spoon. Chop mushrooms and add them to slow cooker. Add ¼ cup soaking liquid to slow cooker and stir until ingredients are well combined. Cover and cook on low setting for 8 to 9 hours.

Place sauce in a food mill and process in batches. Transfer to covered containers and refrigerate or freeze until needed.

If you don't have a food mill, you can puree sauce in a blender. The consistency will be slightly different but the taste will be the same.

Makes: 8 cups

Sausage Puttanesca Sauce

🕐 4–8

Puttanesca — salty, pungent, and fresh — means "streetwalker" style, which gives a tantalizing clue as to its Italian origins. Serve this tasty sauce with your choice of pasta or use it in lasagna. You can double the recipe and use a 6-quart slow cooker. The cooking time remains the same.

1 tablespoon olive oil
2 teaspoons garlic paste or minced garlic
1 pound hot Italian sausage
1 (28-ounce) can whole peeled plum tomatoes, drained and roughly chopped
2 (14.5-ounce) cans petite diced tomatoes, drained
¼ cup capers, rinsed and drained
2 tablespoons pitted and chopped oil-cured kalamata olives
¼ teaspoon salt
2 tablespoons Gourmet Garden Mediterranean Herb and Spice Blend
    (or 1 teaspoon dried oregano and 1 teaspoon dried basil)

Place olive oil in a large nonstick skillet over medium heat. When oil is hot, add garlic and sauté for 30 seconds. Add sausage and break it into bits with a wooden spoon. Cook, stirring frequently, until cooked through. Remove sausage and garlic with a slotted spoon and drain on paper toweling. Transfer sausage and garlic to a 4-quart slow cooker.

Add tomatoes, capers, olives, salt, and seasoning blend to slow cooker. Stir to combine ingredients. Cover slow cooker and cook on low setting for 5½ hours. Stir ingredients, re-cover, and cook an additional 1½ hours.

Transfer to covered containers and refrigerate or freeze until needed.

🕐 You'll find oil-cured kalamata olives where you'd find regular jarred olives in your supermarket. They are olives that have been cured in oil and appear black and shriveled. Kalamata olives have a distinctively pungent flavor. Once opened, store the olives in the refrigerator. They will keep for up to 6 months.

Makes: 6 cups

Peach Chutney

-4

A staple in Indian cuisine, this fruity, sweet and sour chutney should be made at the height of fresh peach season, then frozen in one-cup canning jars for use in Chutney Sauced Cocktail Meatballs (page 129) or as an accompaniment for Rogan Josh (page 44). It also makes a tangy condiment for grilled chicken, beef, or pork.

1 tablespoon butter

½ cup chopped sweet onions, like Vidalia

1 tablespoon garlic paste or finely minced garlic

1 tablespoon gingerroot paste or finely minced gingerroot

1 tablespoon minced jalapeño peppers

1½ teaspoons mustard seeds

¼ teaspoon curry powder

2 cups brown sugar

2 cups cider vinegar

2 pounds fresh freestone peaches (about 6)

½ cup golden raisins

¼ cup dried currants

½ cup peach schnapps or peach nectar

Melt butter in a large nonstick saucepan over medium heat. Add onions, garlic, gingerroot, and jalapeños. Sauté for 3 minutes, stirring frequently. Add mustard seed, curry powder, brown sugar, and vinegar. Stir to combine. Cook for 5 minutes, stirring occasionally.

Meanwhile, bring a medium saucepan of water to boil over high heat. Remove pan from heat and place on a hot pad. Place each peach in hot water for about 30 seconds, remove, and peel. Cut peaches away from pit into ¾-inch slices.

Add peach slices, raisins, currants, and schnapps or nectar to vinegar mixture. Place in a 4-quart slow cooker. Cover slow cooker and cook on low setting for 3 to 4 hours, stirring halfway through cooking time, until sauce is rich and thick. Transfer to 1-cup canning jars and refrigerate for up to 2 weeks or freeze until needed.

You can use two (1-pound) bags frozen peach slices, thawed, if you'd like to make the chutney out of season.

Makes: 8 cups

Pink Banana Butter

 4–8

This is not really butter, but banana lovers will savor its sweet flavor and creamy consistency. Use it for Spicy Ginger Beef (page 35). Or, spread the banana butter on warm muffins. It also makes a great filling between cake layers.

4 cups mashed bananas (about 3½ pounds)
1 cup chopped fresh or frozen strawberries
1 tablespoon melted butter
¼ cup fresh lime juice

Mix bananas, strawberries, butter, and lime juice together in a 4-quart slow cooker. Cook on low setting for 6 to 7 hours, until pink and smooth. Transfer to pint canning jars or other covered containers, and refrigerate or freeze until needed.

Everyone has a banana or two that doesn't get eaten in a timely fashion — not rotten but sort of mushy. Don't throw them out. Peel the overripe banana, wrap it in plastic wrap, and freeze it. When you have enough frozen bananas (about 7 or 8), simple defrost the bananas, scrape away any darkened parts, mash, and use them in this recipe.

Makes: 5 to 6 cups

Beef, Veal, and Lamb

- Spicy Ginger Beef – *Indonesia*
- Beef Bourguignon – *France*
- Hungarian Goulash – *Hungary*
- Irish Stew – *Ireland*
- Russian Beef Stew – *Russia*
- Persian Beef and Rhubarb Khoresh – *Middle East*
- Rogan Josh – *India*
- Neapolitan Genovese – *Italy*
- Chinese Red Cooked Beef – *China*
- Beef and Onion Potjie – *South Africa*
- Sweet and Sour Eye of Round – *Germany*
- Sauerbraten – *Germany*
- Braciole – *Italy*
- Beef Brisket – *USA*
- Hoisin-Ale Braised Short Ribs – *Fusion*
- Sloppy Joes – *USA*
- Catalan Meatballs with Green Olive Sauce – *France*
- Currant-Glazed Corned Beef – *United Kingdom*
- Lemon-Artichoke Veal Stew – *Italy*
- Moroccan Lamb Tagine – *Morocco*
- Lamb in Spicy Peanut Sauce – *Southeast Asia*
- Cape Malay Lamb Curry – *South Africa*
- Braised Lamb Shanks – *Med Rim*

Spicy Ginger Beef

🕐 4–8

This spicy-sweet, Indonesian-inspired beef is best served over coconut rice. To make the rice, simply substitute canned coconut milk for half the water in your favorite rice recipe. You can also serve the dish over Persian Rice (page 121).

½ cup flour

1 teaspoon salt

2 ½ teaspoons black pepper

4 pounds beef stew meat,
    cut into 1½-inch pieces

3 tablespoons olive oil, divided

½ cup chopped sweet onions, like Vidalia

1 dried hot red chile pepper

¼ cup gingerroot paste or
    grated fresh gingerroot

1 tablespoon plus 1 teaspoon garlic paste
    or finely minced garlic

¼ cup fresh lemon juice

¼ cup honey

1 teaspoon Chinese five-spice powder

1 tablespoon dried basil

⅓ cup teriyaki sauce

½ cup orange juice

1 cup Pink Banana Butter (page 33)

Place flour, salt, and ½ teaspoon black pepper in a large zipper bag. Add about 10 pieces of beef to bag, close bag, and shake to coat beef with flour. Shake excess flour off each piece and transfer to a large plate. Repeat process with remaining beef.

Place 1 tablespoon olive oil in a large nonstick skillet over medium heat. When oil is hot, place about one-third of the floured beef pieces in skillet and brown on all sides, about 1 minute total. Transfer beef to a 5-quart slow cooker. Repeat process with remaining beef.

Add onions to skillet and sauté for about 1 minute, until onions have softened slightly and absorbed any flour or meat bits. Transfer onions to slow cooker. Add dried chile pepper to slow cooker.

Whisk together gingerroot paste, garlic, lemon juice, honey, 2 teaspoons black pepper, five-spice powder, basil, teriyaki sauce, and orange juice in a medium bowl. Pour mixture over beef in slow cooker. Cover slow cooker and cook on low setting for 2 hours. Stir ingredients and cook for 3 hours more, until meat is tender but not shredding. Stir in banana butter, reduce heat setting to warm, and hold for 15 minutes, until banana butter melts. Stir and serve.

🕐 The sweet banana butter cuts the spiciness of this dish, adding a sweet finish. If you haven't made the Pink Banana Butter, substitute a cup of sweet jelly or preserves, such as currant jelly or apricot preserves.

Serves: 6 to 8

Beef Bourguignon

 4–8

This classic French dish, originating in the Burgundy district of France, demands a slow simmer in a full-bodied red wine sauce. The manner in which the stew is prepared is more important than using burgundy wine. Any good-to-better red drinking wine will work. Pearl onions, mushrooms, and lardons (fried bacon) are traditional garnishes to the beef.

6 slices bacon, cut into thin strips (about 1 cup)

1 cup flour

2 teaspoons salt

1 teaspoon black pepper

4 pounds sirloin tip roast, cut into ¾- to 1-inch pieces, fat removed

Olive oil, if needed

2 teaspoons garlic paste or finely minced garlic

2 tablespoons tomato paste

1 (10.75-ounce) can Campbell's Golden Mushroom Soup

1 (1-ounce) envelope Lipton Onion Soup Mix

1¼ cups burgundy or other full-bodied red drinking wine

3 tablespoons butter

8 ounces button mushrooms, wiped clean, stems removed, thinly sliced

8 ounces baby bella mushrooms, wiped clean, stems removed, thinly sliced

1 (1-pound) bag frozen pearl onions, thawed and drained

3 tablespoons red currant jelly

Snipped fresh curly parsley

Place bacon in a large nonstick skillet over medium heat. Fry bacon until crispy. Remove from skillet with a slotted spoon. Drain on paper toweling. Store in a small zipper bag in refrigerator until needed. Reserve bacon grease in skillet.

Place flour, salt, and pepper in a large freezer-weight zipper bag. Add meat in batches. Close bag and shake until meat is well coated with flour. Transfer floured meat to a dinner plate. Repeat with remaining pieces of meat.

Heat bacon grease in skillet over medium heat. Brown meat in batches. Transfer browned meat to a 5-quart slow cooker. (If bacon grease cooks away, add 1 to 2 tablespoons olive oil to skillet.)

Place garlic, tomato paste, soup, onion soup mix, and wine in a medium bowl. Whisk until ingredients are well combined. Pour wine mixture into slow cooker. Stir until meat is well coated. (Wine mixture should just barely cover meat. Add more wine if necessary.) Cover slow cooker and cook on low setting for 4 hours.

Meanwhile, melt butter in a large nonstick skillet over medium heat. Add mushrooms and sauté, stirring frequently, for 4 minutes. Add onions and sauté for 1 minute more. Transfer to a covered container and refrigerate until needed.

When meat has cooked for 4 hours, add reserved mushrooms, onions, and bacon to slow cooker. Add red currant jelly. Stir to combine ingredients. Re-cover slow cooker and cook for 1 hour more.

To serve: Sprinkle each portion with parsley before serving. Serve with wide noodles, boiled new potatoes, or garlic bread.

You can freeze this dish in a large covered container for up to 1 month. Place in a 9x13-inch shallow baking dish, cover with aluminum foil, and reheat at 325°F for 30 to 45 minutes. Thin sauce with additional red wine if needed.

Serves: 8 to 10

Hungarian Goulash

 4–8

Hungarian goulash or bogrács gulyás means herdsman's meat. Originally cooked in an iron kettle over an open fire, the dish could contain beef or lamb, as farmers and shepherds contributed what they could. Invading Turks introduced paprika to Hungary in the 16th century. The spice is now considered an essential ingredient in the goulash.

1 teaspoon olive oil

1 (3-pound) boneless chuck roast,
 cut into 1½-inch pieces

½ teaspoon coarse salt

½ teaspoon cracked black pepper

5 cups sliced sweet onions, like Vidalia

¼ cup brown sugar

¼ cup fresh lime juice

½ teaspoon garlic powder

1 teaspoon hot ground mustard powder

1 tablespoon Worcestershire sauce

½ cup ketchup

2 teaspoons paprika

3 large Yukon Gold potatoes,
 peeled and cut into 1½-inch chunks

2 tablespoons cornstarch

Salt and freshly ground black pepper

Sour cream

Place olive oil in a large nonstick skillet over medium heat. Sprinkle meat with salt and pepper. Place meat in skillet in batches and brown on all sides, about 3 minutes. Transfer to a 5- or 6-quart slow cooker. Top meat with onions. Whisk brown sugar, lime juice, garlic powder, mustard powder, Worcestershire sauce, ketchup, and paprika together in a medium bowl. Pour mixture over meat.

Cook meat on low setting for 5 hours. Add potatoes and cook for 1 hour more, until potatoes are cooked through and meat is tender when tested with a knife, but not falling apart. (Hold on warm setting for up to 1½ hours, if necessary.)

With a slotted spoon, transfer meat, onions, and potatoes to a large bowl. Pour all but ¼ cup of the cooking liquid into a small saucepan over medium heat. Place cornstarch in a small bowl. Whisk in ¼ cup remaining cooking liquid to form a smooth paste. Return meat, onions, and potatoes to slow cooker. Cover and reduce heat to warm setting. Add cornstarch mixture to liquid in saucepan and whisk until thickened, about 10 minutes. Season with salt and pepper to taste.

To serve: Place goulash in a large, shallow serving bowl. Pour sauce over goulash and serve with sour cream on the side.

Shred leftover beef and mix it with onions and remaining sauce. Transfer to a covered container and refrigerate or freeze until needed. To serve, reheat beef and sauce in a medium saucepan and serve on hamburger buns with dill pickle slices.

Serves: 6 to 8

Irish Stew

Originally, Irish stew was made from kid (young goat), which was raised primarily for its skin, or mutton from an old sheep no longer deemed useful. Wool-bearing sheep and young lambs were too valuable to sacrifice for dinner. This version of the classic calls for beef, but if your pocketbook allows, you can substitute leg of lamb for a more authentic stew. Whatever meat you use, Irish Stew is traditionally layered as described below.

⅓ cup flour

2½ pounds sirloin tip roast, cut into 1½-inch pieces

Salt and freshly ground black pepper

1½ pounds white new potatoes, cut in half

2 large leeks, white and light green parts only, cut in half lengthwise, washed, and cut
    crosswise into ¾-inch pieces

1 large sweet onion, like Vidalia, cut in half and thinly sliced

1½ cups beef broth

2 teaspoons garlic paste or finely minced garlic

1 teaspoon dried thyme

2 teaspoons Worcestershire sauce

Snipped fresh curly parsley

Place flour in a large zipper bag. Add beef, 5 or 6 pieces at a time, closing bag and shaking it until flour coats beef evenly. Transfer floured beef to a large plate. Season beef with 1 teaspoon salt and ½ teaspoon pepper.

Place half the potatoes in the bottom of a 5-quart slow cooker. Top with half the leeks and half the onions. Place beef pieces atop vegetables. Layer remaining leeks, onions, and potatoes atop meat.

Whisk broth, garlic paste, thyme, and Worcestershire sauce together in a medium bowl. Pour over ingredients in slow cooker. Cover slow cooker and cook on low setting for 6 to 6½ hours, until beef and potatoes are tender.

To serve: Season with salt and pepper to taste. Place each serving in a large, shallow soup bowl. Top with a sprinkling of fresh parsley.

🕐 You can hold stew in slow cooker for up to 3 hours on warm setting.

Serves: 6

Russian Beef Stew

 4–8

The amazing comingling of horseradish and mustard in this otherwise traditional beef stew is a Russian-inspired marriage made in heaven. The addition of sour cream just before serving mellows the tangy sauce and makes it creamy. Serve with new red potatoes or wide egg noodles.

6 tablespoons butter, divided

3 pounds beef stew meat, cut into 2-inch chunks

Salt and freshly ground black pepper

4 teaspoons garlic paste or finely minced garlic

4 cups chopped sweet onions, like Vidalia

1 cup finely chopped baby carrots

1 cup beef broth

1 cup white wine

2 bay leaves

3 tablespoons flour

½ cup prepared horseradish

2 tablespoons Dijon mustard

½ cup sour cream

Snipped fresh curly parsley

Melt 4 tablespoons butter in a large nonstick skillet over medium heat. Brown half the meat, about 30 seconds per side. Transfer meat to a large plate with a slotted spoon. Repeat this process with remaining meat. Season meat with salt and pepper to taste.

Add garlic, onions, and carrots to skillet, and sauté, stirring occasionally, for 5 minutes. Season with salt and pepper to taste. Transfer vegetables to a 4-quart slow cooker. Place browned meat atop vegetables. Mix broth and wine together in a 2-cup measuring cup. Pour mixture over beef and vegetables in slow cooker. Tuck bay leaves into meat mixture. Cover slow cooker and cook on low setting for 7 hours, until beef is tender but not shredding.

Remove beef and vegetables from slow cooker with a slotted spoon and place in a large bowl. Strain liquid through a sieve, reserving juices and placing any strained vegetables in bowl with beef. Place beef and vegetables back in slow cooker. Cover and reduce heat setting to warm.

Melt remaining 2 tablespoons butter in a medium saucepan over medium-low heat. Whisk in flour. Whisk in reserved cooking juices. When mixture comes to a boil, reduce heat to low. Cook, whisking constantly, until sauce thickens, about 10 minutes. Whisk in horseradish and mustard. Season with salt and pepper to taste. Pour horseradish sauce over beef and vegetables in slow cooker. Re-cover and allow flavors to marry on warm setting for at least 1 hour or up to 3 hours.

To serve: Stir sour cream into stew until sauce is creamy. Transfer beef, vegetables, and sauce to a serving bowl, and sprinkle with parsley.

My supermarket reduces the price of Angus beef a day before the package sell-by date. It is a great way to stock your freezer with this usually pricey prime stew beef.

Serves: 6

Persian Beef and Rhubarb Khoresh

 4–8

A khoresh is a delicate, refined Persian stew that may be a combination of meat, poultry, or fish, vegetables, fresh or dried fruits, beans, grains, and even nuts. Traditionally simmered for a long time atop the stove, a khoresh converts wonderfully to a slow cooker. A good Persian cook uses whatever fruits and vegetables are in season. This light and refreshing springtime beef stew showcases fresh rhubarb. Serve with steamed rice or boiled new potatoes.

1 tablespoon olive oil

1½ pounds chuck roast, cut into 1½-inch chunks

4 cups thinly sliced sweet onions, like Vidalia

1½ teaspoons salt

¼ teaspoon black pepper

¼ teaspoon ground turmeric

2 cups snipped fresh parsley

½ cup snipped fresh mint

¼ ground saffron dissolved in 1 tablespoon water (optional)

1 tablespoon tomato paste

1 tablespoon fresh lime juice

1½ cups hot water

2½ cups peeled, diced rhubarb (about 1 pound)

2 tablespoons sugar

1 tablespoon cornstarch

Place oil in a large nonstick skillet over medium heat. When oil is hot, add beef and sauté, stirring frequently, for 2½ minutes. Add onions and sauté, stirring frequently, until meat has browned and onions are soft, about 2 minutes more. Transfer beef and onions to a 4-quart slow cooker.

Add salt, pepper, turmeric, parsley, mint, saffron, tomato paste, lime juice, and hot water. Stir to combine. Cover slow cooker and cook for 4 hours.

Toss rhubarb and sugar in a medium bowl. Add to slow cooker and stir ingredients. Cover and cook for 1½ hours, until meat is tender and rhubarb is cooked through but still firm.

Place cornstarch in a small bowl. Stir in ¼ cup liquid from slow cooker. Stir cornstarch mixture

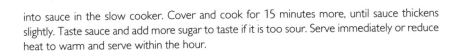

into sauce in the slow cooker. Cover and cook for 15 minutes more, until sauce thickens slightly. Taste sauce and add more sugar to taste if it is too sour. Serve immediately or reduce heat to warm and serve within the hour.

Saffron is a common ingredient in the cuisine of the Middle East, where it is plentiful. Actually the dried stigmas of the crocus flower, entirely harvested by hand, saffron is very expensive. You can omit it in this recipe without sacrificing the unique flavors of the dish. Although turmeric — a member of the ginger family — does not taste like saffron, it is inexpensive, will add the same distinctive yellow coloring to the dish, and adds its own subtle flavor. Substitute turmeric for the saffron if you like.

Serves: 4 to 6

Rogan Josh

 8+

Originating in Kashmir, in northern India, Rogan Josh is a stew, usually made with lamb, which is indigenous to that country. Here in the United States, lamb is a bit pricey, so this version of the traditional highly spiced stew is made with beef. Every Indian family has its own recipe for Rogan Josh, usually handed down, by mother to daughter, throughout the generations. The recipe gets its name from the rich, red color imparted by copious amounts of ground hot red peppers. If you like your food really spicy, add more cayenne pepper. Serve with steamed white rice or Indian naan (flatbread).

1½ teaspoons ground cardamom

2 bay leaves

6 whole cloves

Salt and black pepper

1 (1-inch) stick cinnamon

1 teaspoon ground coriander

2 teaspoons ground cumin

4 teaspoons red paprika

½ teaspoon cayenne pepper

1 tablespoon olive oil

1¾ to 2 pounds beef chuck, cut into 1-inch cubes

2 cups chopped sweet onions, like Vidalia

1 tablespoon gingerroot paste

1 tablespoon garlic paste

1 cup beef broth

¼ cup dried, sweetened coconut, divided

¼ cup slivered almonds, dry-toasted

1 cup plain yogurt, divided

Place cardamom, bay leaves, cloves, ¼ teaspoon black pepper, and cinnamon stick in a small bowl. Set aside. Place coriander, cumin, 1¼ teaspoons salt, paprika, and cayenne pepper in another small bowl. Set aside.

Place olive oil in a large nonstick skillet over medium heat. Add beef cubes and sauté, stirring frequently, for 2 minutes, until meat is browned. Transfer beef to a 2-quart slow cooker with a slotted spoon.

Place cardamom spice mixture in skillet over medium heat and stir for 10 seconds. Add onions and sauté, stirring frequently, for 2 minutes. Add gingerroot and garlic pastes and sauté for 30 seconds, stirring constantly. Add coriander spice mixture and sauté for 30 seconds more. Transfer onion mixture to slow cooker.

Add broth, 2 tablespoons coconut, and almonds to slow cooker. Stir until all ingredients are well mixed. Cover and cook on low setting for 8 hours. Reduce heat to warm setting. Stir in ½ cup yogurt and serve within 15 minutes. Season with salt and pepper to taste.

To serve: Sprinkle each portion with ½ tablespoon coconut and top with a dollop of yogurt.

· ·

🕐 If you don't have gingerroot and garlic pastes *(see Slow Cooking Tips page 145)*, you can make your own by placing 1 tablespoon peeled and chopped gingerroot and 1 tablespoon finely minced garlic in a blender with 2 tablespoons water. Blend until ingredients form a smooth paste. Cardamom, coriander, and cumin are much more fragrant and flavorful if freshly ground. Buy the spices in seed form, which keeps forever, and grind what you need with a mortar and pestle.

Serves: 4

Neapolitan Genovese

 4–8

Virtually unknown outside of the Italian province of Campania, Genovese sauce is thought to have originated in the 16th century. Composed of onions, diced carrots, celery, and parsley, stewed with a cut of beef or veal, a properly prepared Genovese is reminiscent of a fine French onion soup, but with the thick consistency of a Bolognese tomato sauce.

2 tablespoons olive oil

1 (3-pound) chuck roast

3 ounces prosciutto, finely diced (about ½ cup)

3 ounces pancetta, finely diced (about ½ cup)

8 cups halved and thinly sliced sweet onions, like Vidalia (about 2 pounds)

⅓ cup minced celery

⅓ cup minced carrots

⅓ cup snipped fresh flat-leaf parsley

½ teaspoon dried marjoram

1 teaspoon salt

1 teaspoon garlic paste or finely minced garlic

½ cup dry white wine

1 tablespoon cornstarch

1 pound ziti or penne pasta

Grated Parmesan cheese

Freshly ground black pepper

Place oil in a large nonstick saucepan over medium heat. When oil is hot, add chuck roast and brown on all sides, about 3 minutes. Transfer roast to a 4-quart slow cooker.

Add prosciutto, pancetta, onions, celery, carrots, parsley, marjoram, salt, and garlic to saucepan. Cook, stirring frequently, until onions have softened, about 8 to 10 minutes. Transfer onion mixture and juices to slow cooker.

Cook on low setting for 6 hours, until meat is fork-tender. Remove meat from slow cooker and wrap it in aluminum foil. Mix wine and cornstarch together in a small bowl. Add mixture to slow cooker and stir into sauce. Cook sauce on high setting for 45 to 60 minutes, until sauce is thick and slightly dark in color, and onions are creamy.

About 15 minutes before serving, bring a large pot of water to a boil over high heat. Add pasta, reduce heat to medium, and cook pasta until al dente, following package directions. Drain pasta in a colander.

To serve: Slice meat and place on a serving platter. Drizzle meat with sauce. Place pasta in a large bowl. Toss sauce with pasta so that pasta is well coated but not drowning in sauce. Sprinkle pasta liberally with Parmesan cheese and freshly ground black pepper, and serve pasta and meat immediately.

Shred leftover meat, add to any remaining sauce, and mince in a food processor. Serve in a hamburger bun or use as a filling for enchiladas.

Serves: 6

Chinese Red Cooked Beef

Red cooking, or hung shao, *is a Chinese culinary technique that calls for meat to be quickly seared and then slowly simmered in a spicy broth. Supposedly, the "red" color comes from copious amounts of soy sauce in the broth. In this recipe, I've substituted ponzu sauce, a citrus and vinegar–flavored soy sauce, for a lighter, more flavorful broth.*

1 (1¾-pound) skirt steak
1 tablespoon olive oil
1 (1-inch) piece gingerroot, peeled and thinly sliced
3 scallions, halved lengthwise and cut into thirds
½ cup ponzu sauce
1 teaspoon garlic paste or finely minced garlic
1 tablespoon sugar
1 cup water

Cut steak into pieces that will fit into a 1½-quart slow cooker, about 4 inches by 4 inches. Place oil in a large nonstick skillet over medium-high heat. When oil is hot, add steak, searing each side only 15 seconds per side. Transfer seared steak to slow cooker.

Sprinkle gingerroot slices and scallions over beef. Whisk ponzu sauce, garlic, and sugar together in a medium bowl. Whisk in water and pour mixture over beef in slow cooker.

Cover slow cooker and cook on low setting for 3 to 3½ hours, until steak is medium-rare when tested with a sharp knife.

To serve: Remove steak from slow cooker and cut into ½-inch slices. Serve immediately, drizzled with sauce if desired.

You can find ponzu sauce in the Asian section of the international aisle of your supermarket. I look for Angus skirt steak when my supermarket reduces its beef prices for quick sale. Sell-by date is usually the day after I purchase the meat, but if immediately frozen, the meat preserves nicely. Angus beef is usually more tender and flavorful than "choice," and therefore more expensive.

Serves: 4

Beef and Onion Potjie

🕐 4–8

Possibly one of the first slow cookers in the world, a potjie is a South African cast-iron pot that hangs over the coals of an open fire, slowly braising the ingredients therein. And like a slow cooker, the secret to success is all-around heat, slow braising, and not lifting the lid, ensuring that the natural juices create an intense sauce. This South African beef and onion stew tastes even better when made a couple of days ahead and reheated.

2 tablespoons flour

½ teaspoon paprika

Salt and black pepper

1¾ pounds chuck roast,
    cut into 1½- to 2-inch chunks

1 tablespoon olive oil

1½ cups roughly chopped sweet onions,
    like Vidalia

3 tablespoons red wine

¼ cup beef broth

1½ tablespoons tomato paste

1 tablespoon grated fresh orange peel

1 bay leaf

½ stick cinnamon

3 whole cloves

½ (1-pound) package frozen white pearl
    onions, defrosted and drained

Mix flour, paprika, ½ teaspoon salt, and ½ teaspoon pepper together in a small bowl. Place beef chunks in a large bowl. Sprinkle beef with flour mixture and toss until beef is well coated.

Place oil in a large nonstick skillet over medium heat. When oil is hot, add beef and chopped onions. Sauté until beef has browned, about 3 minutes. Mix wine, broth, and tomato paste together in a small bowl. Add to skillet and stir to combine with beef and onions, while deglazing the pan of any burned bits of flour mixture.

Transfer beef mixture to a 2-quart slow cooker. Stir in orange peel, bay leaf, cinnamon stick, and cloves. Cover and cook on low setting for 4 hours. Add pearl onions, stir into beef mixture, cover, and cook for 1 to 1½ hours more, until beef is tender but not falling apart. Remove bay leaf and cinnamon stick. Add salt and pepper to taste before serving.

🍴 Serve this stew with baked, boiled, or mashed potatoes, topping them with the flavorful gravy.

Serves: 3 to 4

Sweet and Sour Eye of Round

 4–8

Eye of round roast is very lean, lacking the marbling of fat found in other cuts of beef. It needs to be braised — covered in liquid — which makes it the perfect cut to use in a slow cooker. Serve with mashed potatoes or rice.

1 tablespoon olive oil

1 (4¾- to 5-pound) eye of round roast

2 large sweet onions, like Vidalia, cut in half and thinly sliced

1 cup ketchup

1 (12-ounce) bottle Bennetts Chili Sauce

⅓ cup red wine vinegar

¼ cup packed brown sugar

2 tablespoons Worcestershire sauce

1 teaspoon dry mustard

1 teaspoon dried oregano

1 teaspoon black pepper

½ teaspoon garlic powder

½ teaspoon chili powder

½ teaspoon ground cloves

¼ teaspoon ground nutmeg

1 teaspoon hot sauce

2 cups water

1 tablespoon cornstarch

Place olive oil in a large nonstick saucepan over medium heat. Add roast and sear on all sides, about 2 minutes. Transfer seared roast to a 5- or 6-quart slow cooker. Top the roast with onions.

Whisk ketchup, chili sauce, vinegar, brown sugar, Worcestershire sauce, dry mustard, oregano, pepper, garlic powder, chili powder, cloves, nutmeg, and hot sauce together in a large bowl. Stir in water. Pour mixture over roast in slow cooker. Cover and cook on low for 6 hours, until roast has cooked through but is still firm.

Remove roast from slow cooker. Cover with aluminum foil. Whisk cornstarch with 2 tablespoons cooking liquid. Add cornstarch mixture to slow cooker and whisk to combine. Re-cover slow cooker, raise heat to high setting, and cook sauce for 15 minutes.

Cut roast into thin slices. Return slices to slow cooker, reduce heat to low setting, re-cover, and cook for 1 hour more, until beef is fork-tender.

To serve: Serve beef slices topped with onions and sauce.

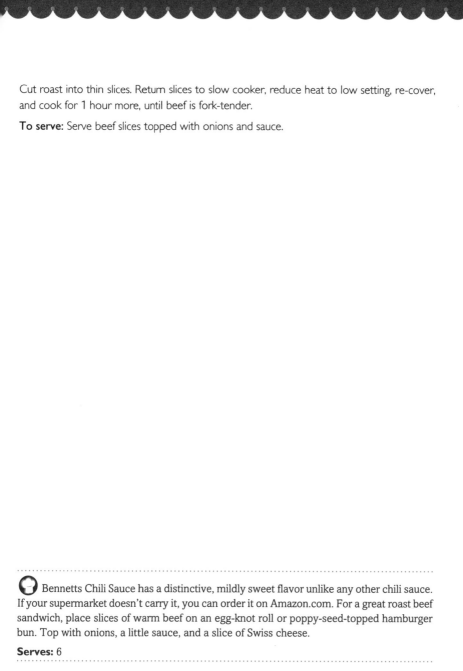

Bennetts Chili Sauce has a distinctive, mildly sweet flavor unlike any other chili sauce. If your supermarket doesn't carry it, you can order it on Amazon.com. For a great roast beef sandwich, place slices of warm beef on an egg-knot roll or poppy-seed-topped hamburger bun. Top with onions, a little sauce, and a slice of Swiss cheese.

Serves: 6

Sauerbraten

 4–8

One of the national dishes of Germany, sauerbraten, or "sour roast," requires two steps in its preparation: marinating for at least 2 to 3 days, then slow cooking for 6 to 8 hours. German settlers brought many versions of this braised pot roast to the Midwest. Some used pork or buffalo meat, but beef rump roast is traditional.

1 (4-pound) rump roast

MARINADE
3 cups halved and sliced sweet onions, like Vidalia
1 stalk celery, chopped
1 large carrot, peeled and chopped
2 bay leaves
4 whole cloves
6 black peppercorns
6 whole allspice seeds
½ teaspoon mustard seeds
½ teaspoon dried thyme leaves
1 cup red wine
1 cup red wine vinegar
2 cups water

Salt and black pepper
3 slices bacon, cut into ½-inch strips
2 cups chopped sweet onions, like Vidalia
1 cup crushed gingersnaps
⅓ cup raisins
1 tablespoon molasses

Two to 3 days ahead: Place rump roast in a large freezer-weight zipper bag. Add onions, celery, carrots, bay leaves, and cloves to bag. Place peppercorns and allspice in a mortar and crush with a pestle, or place spices on a cutting board and crush them by pressing down hard with the side of a large knife blade. Place in a small bowl. Add mustard seeds and thyme, and stir to combine. Sprinkle spices over roast in bag. Mix wine, vinegar, and water together in a 4-cup measuring cup. Pour over roast. Close zipper on bag. Place zipped bag inside another freezer-weight zipper bag and massage until marinade ingredients are well mixed and covering roast. Refrigerate until needed, massaging bag several times each day.

To cook: Remove roast from marinade. Place on a cutting board and pat dry with paper toweling. Pour marinade through a strainer into a large measuring cup. Discard vegetables and spices and all but 1 cup marinade. Set marinade aside until needed. Sprinkle all sides of roast with I teaspoon salt and ½ teaspoon pepper.

Place a large nonstick skillet over medium heat. Add bacon and cook until crispy, about 3 minutes. Remove bacon with a slotted spoon and drain on paper toweling. Add roast to skillet and brown on all sides. Place browned roast in a 4-quart slow cooker. Top with bacon and onions. Place reserved marinade in a microwave-safe container, microwave it for 1 minute, then pour marinade over roast. Cover slow cooker and cook for 6 to 8 hours, until meat is tender when tested with a knife, but not shredding.

Remove roast from cooking liquid and place on a cutting board. Wrap tightly with aluminum foil. Turn slow cooker up to high setting. Add gingersnaps, raisins, and molasses. Cover and cook for 10 minutes, until sauce has thickened.

To serve: Cut roast into thick slices and place on a serving platter. Spoon sauce over sauerbraten and season with salt and pepper to taste. Serve remaining sauce on the side.

Serve with potato dumplings, potato pancakes, boiled new potatoes, spaetzle, or red cabbage. The crushed gingersnaps thicken the liquid of the sauce.

Serves: 6 to 8

Braciole

-4

Southern Italians rarely had access to tender cuts of beef, usually using bottom round for their long-braised braciole, an inventive dish that makes the most of a small amount of meat. In the United States, however, what is sold as "bottom round" or "beef for braciole" is not as marbled as its counterpart in Italy. Since a little marbling is prerequisite for tender braciole, look for any thinly cut steak streaked with fat — even chuck — when making this recipe.

1½ pounds thinly sliced New York strip steak (4 slices)

4 thin slices prosciutto

2 cloves garlic, finely minced

2 tablespoons pine nuts

2 tablespoons raisins

½ cup snipped fresh flat-leaf parsley

1¼ cups freshly grated Parmesan cheese, divided

Salt and freshly ground black pepper

2 cups Real Deal Italian Meatless Sauce (page 30)

¾ pound penne pasta

Up to 1 month ahead: Trim excess fat from edges of steak slices. Place each steak slice between 2 large sheets of waxed paper and pound with a mallet until steak is ¼ inch thick. Place 1 slice prosciutto atop each pounded steak slice. Sprinkle each steak with equal amounts of garlic, pine nuts, raisins, parsley, and ¾ cup Parmesan cheese. Roll up each slice like a sausage, tucking in the sides as you roll. Tie each rolled steak with kitchen string, crosswise and lengthwise. Wrap each roll tightly in plastic wrap and place in a freezer-weight zipper bag. Freeze until needed.

To cook: Defrost braciole rolls and remove each from plastic wrap. Coat a 2-quart slow cooker with vegetable cooking spray. Place braciole rolls in slow cooker. Pour tomato sauce evenly atop rolls. Cover slow cooker and cook on low setting for 3 to 4 hours, until meat has cooked through and sauce is bubbly.

Bring a large pot of water to a boil over high heat. Cook penne to al dente according to package directions, about 8 minutes. Drain pasta. Remove braciole from sauce, and cut and remove strings. Toss drained penne and sauce together in a large bowl.

To serve: Divide sauced penne among 4 individual pasta bowls. Top each with a braciole. Sprinkle each serving with 2 tablespoons grated Parmesan cheese.

Some supermarkets sell thin cuts of steak, but to get really thin slices — round, chuck, skirt, strip, or flank — have a butcher cut them for you.

Serves: 4

Beef Brisket

 4–8

Cosmetologist Dana Munn is not only a great cook in her own right, but she picks up some great recipes from her clients as well. She shares this simple combination of ingredients, which transforms brisket into an otherworldly taste sensation.

1 (4- to 4½-pound) beef brisket
1 tablespoon olive oil
1 (14-ounce) can whole berry cranberry sauce
½ cup orange juice
1 (1-ounce) envelope Lipton Onion Soup Mix

Cut brisket in half, crosswise, into 2 similarly sized pieces. Place oil in a large nonstick skillet over medium heat. When oil is hot, sear both sides of each brisket piece, about 30 seconds per side. Transfer brisket pieces to a dinner plate.

Mix cranberry sauce, orange juice, and onion soup mix together in a medium bowl. Place 1 piece of brisket in a 5-quart slow cooker. Spoon half the cranberry mixture over brisket. Place remaining piece of brisket atop the other. Spoon remaining cranberry mixture over brisket.

Cover slow cooker and cook on low setting for 5 hours. Transfer meat to a cutting board. Slice brisket against the grain into ¼-inch slices. Return brisket slices to slow cooker, making sure they are covered with sauce. Re-cover slow cooker and cook on low setting for 2 hours more, until meat is fork-tender but not shredding.

The brisket is great served with roasted potatoes, onions, and carrots. Simply toss 2 cups of each, cut into 1½-inch pieces, with 1 tablespoon olive oil. Place on a nonstick baking sheet in a 350°F oven for the final hour the brisket is cooking. You can also serve the brisket with rice or orzo.

Serves: 8

Hoisin-Ale Braised Short Ribs

 4–8

The oldest form of beer, ale is fruitier and more full-bodied than lager. Ales come in many forms. I used pale ale in this recipe. Hoisin sauce, a soy-based sauce commonly used in Chinese cooking, has a unique sweet, salty, spicy flavor that can't be duplicated using anything else.

4 to 4½ pounds beef short ribs
Salt and freshly ground black pepper
1 tablespoon olive oil
1 head garlic (12 to 15 cloves), cloves peeled and crushed
1 (1½-inch) piece gingerroot, peeled and sliced ¼-inch thick
1 (12-ounce) bottle ale
3 tablespoons rice wine vinegar
¾ cup bottled hoisin sauce

Season all sides of ribs liberally with salt and pepper. Place oil in a large nonstick skillet over medium heat. Working in 2 batches, sear ribs on all sides. Transfer seared ribs to a 5-quart slow cooker.

Pour off all but 1 tablespoon fat and drippings. Add garlic and gingerroot and sauté, stirring constantly, for about 2 minutes. Transfer garlic and gingerroot to slow cooker with a slotted spoon.

Add ale and vinegar to slow cooker. Cook on low setting for 4½ to 5 hours, until meat is tender and pulling away from the bone. Remove ribs from slow cooker. Cut away meat from bone, removing any visible gristle.

Pour broth through a strainer into a large bowl. Return broth to slow cooker. Stir in hoisin sauce. Return boneless ribs to slow cooker. Cover and reduce heat setting to warm. Hold on warm for at least 30 minutes or up to 2 hours.

To serve: Transfer short ribs to a serving platter. Season with salt and pepper to taste. Transfer sauce to a medium pitcher or bowl. Serve short ribs drizzled with sauce.

If you have a stovetop-safe slow cooker insert, sear ribs in it, instead of a skillet. Wipe out any excess fat or drippings before returning short ribs to insert and proceed with recipe as written.

Serves: 4

Sloppy Joes

 4–8

How this sandwich filling got its name is still a mystery, although many credit it as an invention of Sloppy Joe's Bar in Havana, Cuba. If true, the original was probably picadillo, a distant cousin of the Americanized version. The ideal stateside Sloppy Joe is sweet and spicy at the same time, with a thick, rich sauce, and so is this recipe!

1 pound spicy pork sausage

1½ pounds lean ground beef

1 cup chopped sweet onions

½ cup chopped red bell pepper

1 (6-ounce) can tomato paste with basil, garlic, and oregano

½ cup ketchup

¼ cup firmly packed brown sugar

2 tablespoons cider vinegar

2 tablespoons Dijon mustard

1 tablespoon chili powder

1 tablespoon Worcestershire sauce

½ teaspoon salt

Crumble sausage in a large nonstick skillet over medium heat. Sauté, stirring frequently, until browned, about 5 minutes. Drain in a colander. Add ground beef, onions, and bell peppers to skillet. Sauté, stirring frequently, for 5 minutes or until beef is browned. Drain in a colander.

Transfer sausage and beef mixture from colander to a 4-quart slow cooker. Add tomato paste, ketchup, brown sugar, vinegar, mustard, chili powder, Worcestershire sauce, and salt. Stir to combine ingredients.

Cover and cook on low setting for 4 hours. Stir mixture, re-cover, and turn heat setting to warm until serving, up to 2 hours.

Usually Sloppy Joes are served on hamburger-style buns. You can make Sloppy Joe Sliders by serving them on White Dollar Rolls (found at Walmart Superstores) or other 3-inch-diameter rolls.

Serves: 8 to 10

Catalan Meatballs with Green Olive Sauce 4–8

A specialty of the Roussillon area of southeastern France, which has a heavy Spanish influence from its shared border of the Pyrenees, these beef and sausage meatballs are swaddled in a savory sauce of tomatoes, olives, and sopressata. Locals eat the sauce-topped meatballs with cooked white beans, but new red or white potatoes are wonderful as well.

8 ounces lean ground beef

1 pound sweet Italian pork sausages, casings removed

5 teaspoons garlic paste or finely minced garlic

2 tablespoons snipped fresh flat-leaf parsley

Pinch dried thyme

Salt and freshly ground black pepper

2 eggs, beaten

¼ cup flour

2 tablespoons olive oil, divided

1½ cups chopped sweet onions, like Vidalia

1 (14.5-ounce) can petite-cut tomatoes, with juices

2 ounces sopressata or prosciutto, cut into small dice

¼ teaspoon crushed red pepper flakes

⅛ teaspoon ground cinnamon

½ teaspoon paprika

1½ cups water

¾ cup pitted green olives without pimento

Crumble ground beef and sausages into a large bowl. Add garlic, parsley, thyme, and salt and pepper to taste. Mix ingredients together with clean hands. Add eggs and mix well.

Place flour on a dinner plate. Form mixture into golf-ball-size meatballs and roll each in flour. Set on a clean plate. (Meatballs will adhere together loosely.) Repeat with remaining meat mixture.

Place 1 tablespoon oil in a large nonstick skillet over medium heat. Add half the meatballs and sauté, turning meatballs frequently until they are browned, about 4 minutes. Transfer meatballs to a 4-quart slow cooker. Repeat process with remaining oil and meatballs.

Add onions to skillet and sauté for 2 minutes. Stir in tomatoes, sopressata, red pepper flakes, cinnamon, paprika, and water. Bring to a boil over medium heat. Reduce heat to medium-low and simmer sauce for 5 minutes.

Sprinkle olives over meatballs in slow cooker. Pour sauce over meatballs. Cover slow cooker and cook on low setting for 4 hours.

Sopressata is Italian slow-aged, dried salami. You can find it at your supermarket's deli counter. You can substitute prosciutto.

Serves: 4 to 6

Currant-Glazed Corned Beef

 4–8

Referred to in England as boiled beef dinner, corned beef is a staple meal all around the United Kingdom. Before the days of refrigeration, beef was cured in salt brine for preservation. The term "corned" refers to the corns, or grains, of salt in which it is cured.

1 (3¾- to 4-pound) flat-cut corned beef brisket

2 tablespoons snipped fresh mint

3 tablespoons brown sugar

1½ tablespoons cider vinegar

¼ cup plus 1 tablespoon orange juice, divided

2 dried red hot peppers

4 whole cloves

8 thin sweet onion slices, like Vidalia

4 peeled white sweet potatoes, cut into 1½-inch chunks

2 cups baby carrots

½ cup heavy whipping cream

3 tablespoons prepared horseradish

⅓ cup red currant jelly

½ tablespoon Grand Marnier or other orange liqueur

Rinse corned beef and dry with paper toweling. Place in a 5-quart stovetop-proof slow cooker, fat-side down, and brown for 2 minutes. Turn corned beef and brown other side for 2 minutes. Remove from heat and sprinkle mint over corned beef.

Whisk together brown sugar, vinegar, and ¼ cup orange juice. Pour over corned beef. Add peppers and cloves to slow cooker, on either side of corned beef. Place onions over corned beef like a blanket. Add water to just cover corned beef (about 5½ cups). Cover slow cooker and cook on low setting for 5½ hours. Add sweet potatoes and carrots to slow cooker, immersing them in the liquid. Re-cover and cook for 1 more hour, until carrots and potatoes are fork-tender.

Meanwhile, whip cream until soft peaks form. Fold in horseradish. Refrigerate until needed.

To serve: Place jelly, 1 tablespoon orange juice, and Grand Marnier in a small saucepan over medium-low heat. Stirring constantly, cook until jelly has melted, about 1 minute. Transfer corned beef to a serving platter with 2 firm spatulas. Drizzle glaze over corned beef. Cut corned beef into slices. Remove vegetables from slow cooker with a slotted spoon and place around perimeter of corned beef. Serve immediately with horseradish cream on the side.

White sweet potatoes can be found in the autumn farmers' markets in many areas of the country. If you can't find them, substitute small, white new potatoes.

Serves: 6 to 8

Lemon-Artichoke Veal Stew

 4–8

French chefs hired by Italian nobles devised this tasty stew, which utilizes the artichokes of Sicily and the lemons of Ravello. Italy grows one billion pounds of artichokes a year.

½ cup flour
1¼ teaspoons salt, divided
½ teaspoon black pepper, divided
3 pounds veal stew meat, cut into 2- to 2½-inch cubes
6 tablespoons olive oil, divided
1 cup chopped sweet onions, like Vidalia
4 teaspoons garlic paste or finely minced garlic
½ teaspoon crushed red pepper flakes
4 teaspoons freshly grated lemon peel
1 (13.75-ounce) can whole artichoke hearts, rinsed, drained, and quartered
6 tablespoons white wine
1½ cups chicken broth
¼ cup fresh lemon juice
2 large eggs
½ cup snipped fresh flat-leaf parsley, divided
1 pound wide egg noodles

Place flour, ½ teaspoon salt, and ¼ teaspoon pepper in a large zipper bag. Add veal to bag, about 5 pieces at a time. Shake bag so that flour coats veal. Transfer flour-dusted veal to a large plate. (Shake off any excess flour.)

Place 2 tablespoons oil in a large nonstick skillet over medium heat. When oil is hot, add about one-third of the veal cubes. Brown veal about 30 seconds per side. Transfer veal to a 4-quart slow cooker. Repeat browning process two more times, adding 2 tablespoons oil each time and transferring browned veal to slow cooker.

Add onions, garlic, crushed red pepper, lemon peel, ½ teaspoon salt, ¼ teaspoon pepper, and artichokes to skillet. Sauté, stirring constantly, for 1 minute. Add wine and sauté, stirring constantly for 1 minute. Add broth and lemon juice and bring to a boil, about 1 minute. Pour mixture over veal in slow cooker. Stir ingredients.

Cover slow cooker and cook on low setting for 4½ to 5 hours. Transfer veal and artichokes to a large bowl with a slotted spoon. Cover bowl with aluminum foil. Whisk eggs, ½ teaspoon salt, and ¼ cup parsley together until frothy. Whisk egg mixture into liquid remaining in slow cooker. Cover slow cooker and cook sauce on high for 10 minutes. Transfer veal and artichokes back to slow cooker. Stir to combine ingredients. Cover and cook on high for 10 minutes more.

Meanwhile, bring a large pot of water to a boil over medium-high heat. Cook noodles to al dente according to package directions. Drain noodles in a colander.

To serve: Divide noodles among 6 large pasta bowls or dinner plates. Top with equal portions of veal stew with sauce. Sprinkle each serving with remaining parsley and serve.

Once veal has cooked through, you can hold it on warm for up to 1 hour before finishing the sauce.

Serves: 6

Moroccan Lamb Tagine

 4–8

Your taste buds will be transported to Marrakesh with this savory lamb stew ubiquitous in the region. Tagine, a slow-cooked stew that is braised at low temperatures, is named after the heavy clay pot in which it is cooked in North Africa. Tagine requires a long list of spices for the rub — great to have in your kitchen stash — and you must marinate the lamb overnight.

MARINADE

1 teaspoon coarse salt
¼ teaspoon cayenne pepper
¾ teaspoon garlic powder
2 teaspoons paprika
¼ teaspoon turmeric
½ teaspoon ground cumin
1 teaspoon ground cinnamon
¾ teaspoon ground coriander
½ teaspoon ground ginger
¼ teaspoon ground cloves
½ teaspoon ground cardamom
2 teaspoons dried mint leaves

1¾ to 2 pounds boneless leg of lamb, cut into 1-inch pieces
¼ cup olive oil, divided
3 cups roughly chopped (1-inch) sweet onions, like Vidalia
3 cups peeled, seeded butternut squash chunks (1-inch pieces)
4 teaspoons garlic paste or finely minced garlic
1 tablespoon gingerroot paste or finely minced gingerroot
1 lemon
1½ tablespoons honey
1 (14.5-ounce) can petite diced tomatoes, drained, rinsed, and drained again
1 (19-ounce) can chickpeas, drained
¾ cup pitted prunes
¾ cup dried apricots
¾ cup chicken broth
¼ cup orange juice
Mint sauce (bottled)

One day ahead: Mix salt, cayenne pepper, garlic powder, paprika, turmeric, cumin, cinnamon, coriander, ginger, cloves, cardamom, and mint leaves together in a small bowl. Place lamb in a large freezer-weight zipper bag. Add spice mixture and close bag. Shake bag until lamb pieces are well coated with herbs and spices. Add 2 tablespoons olive oil to bag. Close bag and manipulate lamb pieces until well coated with oil, herbs, and spices. Refrigerate until needed.

To cook: Place 1 tablespoon oil in a large nonstick skillet over medium heat. Add lamb pieces and sauté until browned, about 3 to 4 minutes. Transfer to a 5-quart slow cooker. Add remaining 1 tablespoon oil to skillet. Add onions and squash, and sauté for 3 minutes. Add garlic and gingerroot pastes. Sauté for 3 minutes more. Transfer vegetable mixture to slow cooker.

Grate lemon peel with a microplane grater. Squeeze juice from lemon. Add juice (2 to 3 tablespoons) and grated lemon peel (about 1 teaspoon) to slow cooker. Add honey, tomatoes, chickpeas, prunes, apricots, broth, and orange juice to slow cooker. Stir until ingredients are well combined. Cover slow cooker and cook on low setting for 4 to 4½ hours, until lamb is tender and squash is cooked through. Reduce heat to warm setting and hold for up to 1 hour.

To serve: Serve each portion in a large shallow soup bowl. Lace tagine with mint sauce to taste. The tagine stands alone as an entrée, but you can serve it with a side of couscous or rice if you'd like.

Don't let the long ingredient list put you off making this tasty dish — the spice rub accounts for nearly half. If you are missing one or two of the spice-rub ingredients, the stew will still come out fine.

Serves: 6

Lamb in Spicy Peanut Sauce

 4–8

This Southeast Asian–sauced lamb calls for spicy brown bean sauce, a robust sauce made from fermented soybeans, sugar, sherry, garlic, and other spices. Along with fish sauce — a salty sauce essential to much of the cuisine of the region — it can be found in the international section of your supermarket.

¼ cup unsalted, dry-roasted peanuts

1½ tablespoons sesame seeds

1 tablespoon canola oil

3 teaspoons garlic paste or finely minced garlic

¼ cup spicy brown bean sauce

1 tablespoon tomato paste

1 tablespoon fish sauce

1 tablespoon peanut butter

1 cup warm water

1 tablespoon sugar

½ cup flour

1¾ pounds boneless leg of lamb, cut into 1-inch pieces

2 tablespoons olive oil

Up to 1 week ahead: Dry-toast peanuts in a small nonstick skillet over medium heat for about 3 minutes, or until they are fragrant and browned slightly. Transfer to a food processor and pulse until peanuts are finely chopped. Set aside.

Place sesame seeds in skillet and dry-toast for 1 to 2 minutes, stirring constantly, until seeds have browned slightly. Remove skillet from heat and set aside.

Place canola oil in a medium nonstick saucepan over medium-low heat. When oil is hot, add garlic, bean sauce, tomato paste, and fish sauce. Stir to combine. Whisk together peanut butter, water, and sugar in a small bowl until smooth. Whisk peanut butter liquid into sauce mixture in saucepan. Increase heat to medium-high and bring to a boil, stirring constantly. Reduce heat to low and simmer for 2 minutes, stirring occasionally. Remove from heat and set aside or place in a covered container and refrigerate until needed. (If refrigerated, reheat sauce in a nonstick saucepan on low before proceeding with recipe.)

To cook: Place flour in a large zipper bag. Add lamb pieces, in batches, shaking until pieces are coated with flour. Shake off excess flour and place pieces on a dinner plate. Place olive oil in a large nonstick skillet over medium heat. When oil is hot, add half the lamb pieces and sauté until browned on all sides, about 1 to 2 minutes. Transfer lamb with a slotted spoon to a 1½- or 2-quart slow cooker. Repeat with remaining lamb pieces. Sprinkle ground peanuts and dry-toasted sesame seeds over lamb in slow cooker.

Pour spicy peanut sauce over lamb, poking any exposed lamb into the sauce. Cover slow cooker and cook on low setting for 5 hours, until lamb is fork-tender.

You can hold the lamb on warm setting for up to 3 hours. Serve with coconut rice. (To make coconut rice, simply replace half the water needed to cook your favorite rice with coconut milk.)

Serves: 6

Cape Malay Lamb Curry

 4–8

In the 17th century, Indonesians were brought to Cape Town, South Africa, to work as slaves on the farms of the western Cape. Known as Cape Malays, they carried with them a spicy-sweet cuisine that has become an enduring favorite in the region and beyond.

3 tablespoons olive oil, divided

6 cups halved and thinly sliced sweet onions, like Vidalia

1 tablespoon garlic paste or finely minced garlic

2 pounds boneless leg of lamb, cleaned of all fat and cut into 1½-inch pieces

¼ teaspoon salt

1 tablespoon Thai red curry paste

2 teaspoons Garden Gourmet Thai Herb

1 teaspoon gingerroot paste or peeled and grated gingerroot

½ teaspoon turmeric

¼ cup fresh lemon juice

1 tablespoon tamarind syrup

½ teaspoon salt

2 tablespoons Coco Lopez Cream of Coconut

1 cup water

Place 2 tablespoons oil in a large nonstick skillet over medium heat. Add onions and sauté, stirring frequently, for 4 minutes. Add garlic and cook for 4 minutes more, stirring frequently. Transfer onions and garlic to a 4-quart slow cooker.

Add 1 tablespoon oil to skillet. Sprinkle lamb with salt. Add half the lamb pieces to the skillet and brown them over medium heat, about 2 minutes. Remove lamb with a slotted spoon and place in slow cooker. Add remaining lamb pieces to skillet and repeat browning process.

Place red curry paste, herb paste, gingerroot, turmeric, lemon juice, tamarind syrup, salt, cream of coconut, and water in a medium bowl. Whisk ingredients into a smooth sauce. Pour sauce into slow cooker. Stir to combine ingredients.

Cover slow cooker and cook on low setting for 4½ to 5½ hours, until lamb is fork-tender. Serve curry with steamed white rice.

Thai red curry paste is made from ground red hot chile peppers. Tamarind syrup, made from the fruit of the tamarind tree, is like the lemon juice of Indonesia. You can find both ingredients in the international section of your supermarket. Coco Lopez is a thick, sweetened coconut cream, often used in tropical drinks. You can find it in the beverage section of your supermarket.

Serves: 4

Braised Lamb Shanks

 4–8

Trimming every bit of fat from the lamb shanks is a laborious task, but the end result is worth every minute of effort. After hours of braising in this lemon-tomato-mint sauce, the tender, succulent lamb falls off the bone and melts in your mouth. Serve the lamb with Persian Rice (page 121).

3 large lamb shanks (about 3 pounds)
2 tablespoons olive oil, divided
3 cups chopped onions
2 teaspoons garlic paste or finely minced garlic
1 teaspoon salt
½ teaspoon black pepper
1 teaspoon ground turmeric
1 (8-ounce) can tomato sauce
6 tablespoons fresh lemon juice
½ cup snipped fresh mint
3 Granny Smith apples, peeled, cored, and sliced

Trim all fat from lamb shanks and discard. Place 1 tablespoon oil in a large nonstick skillet over medium heat. When oil is hot, add lamb shanks and sear until browned, about 3 minutes. Transfer shanks to a 5-quart slow cooker.

Add remaining 1 tablespoon oil to skillet. Add onions, garlic, salt, pepper, and turmeric. Sauté onions over medium heat, stirring frequently, until they are a dark golden color, about 5 minutes. Stir in tomato sauce, lemon juice, and mint. Pour mixture over lamb shanks in slow cooker.

Cover slow cooker and cook on low setting for 6 hours. Place apple slices atop lamb mixture. Re-cover slow cooker and cook for 1½ hours more, until lamb has fallen off the bone and apples have cooked down. Remove shank bones, stir, and serve. Or hold on warm setting for up to 1 hour.

You'll have about one pound of fat from the trimmed lamb shanks. Once the bones are discarded, you'll end up with slightly less than a pound of actual meat. To serve 6, you can add another shank or two and not have to increase the sauce proportions.

Serves: 4

Pork and Poultry

- Brown Sugar Pork Loin Roast – *Caribbean*
- Autumn Harvest Pork Roast – *USA*
- Cuban-Chinese Barbecued Pork Tenderloins – *Cuba*
- Pulled Pork Tenderloin with North Carolina Barbecue Battle Sauces – *USA*
- Slow-Roasted Chipotle Pork Soft Tacos – *Mexico*
- Shredded Pork and Sauerkraut Sammies – *Germany*
- Greek Pork Chops – *Greece*
- Pork Chops and Onions in Gado Gado Sauce – *Indonesia*
- Russian Cherry Orchard Pork Stew – *Russia*
- Indochine Pineapple Pork Stew – *Southeast Asia*
- Hoisin-Ginger Barbecued Baby Back Ribs – *China*
- Mississippi Barbecued Country-Style Ribs – *USA*
- Honey-Baked Ham with Cumberland Sauce – *USA*
- Brats 'n' Beer – *Germany*
- Lemon Chardonnay Chicken Florentine – *France*
- Sun-Dried Tomato and Mushroom–Sauced Chicken – *Italy*
- Herbed Chicken Dijon – *France*
- Island Citrus Chicken – *Caribbean*
- Chicken Marengo – *Italy*
- Chicken and Sweet Potato Stew – *Africa*
- Med-Rim Chicken – *Med Rim*
- Jamaican Jerk Chicken – *Caribbean*
- Fruited Chicken – *Mexico*
- Lebanese Orange-Apricot Chicken – *Med Rim*
- Chinese Roast Chicken – *USA/China Fusion*
- Turkey Breast with Orange-Cranberry Sauce – *USA*

Brown Sugar Pork Loin Roast

 4–8

Reminiscent of slow-roasted pork served on a Caribbean island with the background music of steel drums, this sweet and spicy dish welcomes an accompanying tray of icy margaritas.

2 teaspoons salt

½ teaspoon black pepper

1 teaspoon ground cumin

1 teaspoon chili powder

1 teaspoon ground cinnamon

1 (2½- to 3-pound) pork loin roast

2 tablespoons olive oil

1 cup packed dark brown sugar

2 tablespoons garlic paste or finely minced garlic

1 tablespoon Louisiana hot sauce or other favorite hot sauce

Mix together salt, pepper, cumin, chili powder, and cinnamon in a small bowl. Sprinkle seasoning mixture over all sides of pork, then rub it in well.

Place oil in a large nonstick skillet over medium heat. When oil is hot, add pork and sear on all sides and ends, about 30 seconds per side. Transfer to a 4-quart slow cooker.

Mix brown sugar, garlic paste, and hot sauce together in a medium bowl to form a paste. Spread the paste over the entire top of the pork roast. Cover slow cooker and cook on low setting for 4 hours. Open slow cooker and turn roast over with a sturdy fork. Re-cover slow cooker and cook for 1 hour more, until pork is cooked through and tender but not shredding.

To serve: Slice pork and drizzle with brown sugar sauce from the slow cooker. Serve remaining sauce on the side.

Instead of serving immediately, you can cook pork up to two days ahead. Refrigerate pork in the sauce in a covered container. To serve: Skim off accumulated fat with a spoon and transfer pork and sauce to a deep baking dish so that sauce covers pork. Cover dish with foil and place in the oven at 325°F for about 30 minutes, or until heated through. Continue with serving instructions above.

Serves: 4 to 6

Autumn Harvest Pork Roast

 4–8

Sauced with the fruits of a fall harvest — apples and cranberries — this pork dish is packed with flavor and is as colorful as an autumn day.

½ tablespoon olive oil

1 (2- to 2½-pound) boneless pork loin rib end roast

1 (12-ounce) package frozen Stouffer's Harvest Apples, thawed

1 (14-ounce) can whole berry cranberry sauce

1 cup Catalina salad dressing

2 tablespoons Lipton's Onion Soup Mix

Place oil in a large nonstick skillet over medium heat. When oil is hot, add pork loin and brown all sides, about 3 minutes. Transfer pork to a 4-quart slow cooker.

Microwave apples according to manufacturer's instructions (about 5 minutes). Mix cranberry sauce, salad dressing, onion soup mix, and apples together in a medium bowl. Pour mixture over pork loin. Cover and cook on low setting for 4 hours.

To serve: Thinly slice pork and serve topped with fruit sauce. Place remaining sauce in a bowl and offer it on the side.

Serve pork with fluffy white rice. Top the rice with fruit sauce if desired.

Serves: 4 to 6

Cuban-Chinese Barbecued Pork Tenderloins 4–8

A common sight hanging in the windows of Chinese restaurants are pork tenderloins that have been roasted with honey, hoisin sauce, five-spice powder, garlic, sugar, and soy sauce. You wouldn't expect to see this combination in Cuba, where pork is the most plentiful meat, but you would be wrong. In the nineteenth century, hundreds of Chinese laborers worked in Cuba, bringing this flavorful combination to the island. This recipe adapts the classic for your slow cooker.

3 tablespoons soy sauce

3 tablespoons cream sherry

2 tablespoons hoisin sauce

¼ cup black bean dip

2 tablespoons Chinese five-spice powder

2 tablespoons garlic paste or finely minced garlic

3 tablespoons sugar

¼ cup honey

2 (1¼-pound) pork tenderloins

Mix soy sauce, sherry, hoisin sauce, bean dip, five-spice powder, garlic, sugar, and honey in a medium bowl. Rinse tenderloins and pat dry with paper toweling. Spoon sauce over both sides of each tenderloin. Place tenderloins in a 1½-quart or 2-quart slow cooker. Pour remaining sauce over pork. Cover and cook on low setting for 4 hours, until pork has cooked through but is not shredding.

To serve: Remove tenderloins and cut into ½-inch slices. Drizzle sauce over pork and serve immediately.

Pork tenderloins usually come two to a package. You'll find great prices at one of the price clubs, like Sam's, BJ's, or Costco, or look for sales at your local supermarket.

Serves: 6 to 8

Pulled Pork Tenderloin

 4–8

North Carolinians are justifiably proud of their pulled pork — usually a whole pig slow-cooked outside over hot coals. This recipe, slow-cooked inside in any weather, uses pork tenderloin, which provides the best meat yield with minimum fat content. The sauce war carries on, however, no matter how the pork is cooked. The eastern part of the state prefers a spicy vinegar sauce, while the western mountain region insists on a sweeter red sauce. You be the judge.

1 tablespoon olive oil

Salt and black pepper

1 (5-pound) package pork tenderloins

3 large sweet onions, like Vidalia, cut in half and thinly sliced

⅔ cup ketchup

⅔ cup chicken broth

4 teaspoons garlic paste or finely minced garlic

¼ cup apple cider vinegar

2 tablespoons Worcestershire sauce

1 teaspoon chili powder

½ teaspoon dry mustard

½ teaspoon Tabasco sauce

Place olive oil in a large nonstick skillet over medium heat. Season tenderloins with salt and pepper. Place tenderloins in skillet and sear all sides, about 2 minutes total. Transfer tenderloins to a 5- or 6-quart slow cooker. Top with onions.

Whisk ketchup, broth, garlic, vinegar, Worcestershire sauce, chili powder, dry mustard, and Tabasco sauce together in a medium bowl. Pour mixture over tenderloins. Cook on low setting for 4 to 5 hours, until tenderloins can be shredded with a fork.

Remove tenderloins from sauce. Shred or "pull" with a fork.

To serve: Serve pork, sprinkled with choice of Battle Sauces *(see recipes next page)*, on toasted Kaiser or hamburger rolls. Top with coleslaw if desired.

You can hold pork, once shredded, for up to 2 hours. Return pulled pork to sauce in slow cooker and reduce heat setting to warm. The pork will take on the flavor of the cooking sauce more intensely, so you may want to serve the Battle Sauces on the side or eliminate them.

Serves: 4 to 6

North Carolina Barbecue Battle Sauces

The Hatfields and the McCoys had nothin' on the folks of North Carolina when it came to feuding. The battle over the "proper" barbecue sauce for pulled pork in this southern state goes on to this day.

EASTERN NORTH CAROLINA BARBECUE SAUCE

1 cup apple cider vinegar

1 teaspoon salt

1 teaspoon cayenne pepper

1 tablespoon crushed red pepper flakes

1 tablespoon freshly ground black pepper

Two days ahead: Place all ingredients in a glass jar. Secure lid and shake well. Refrigerate for 2 days to allow flavors to marry. Serve at room temperature.

 Sauce will keep, refrigerated, for up to one month.　　　　**Makes:** 1 cup

WESTERN NORTH CAROLINA BARBECUE SAUCE

2 tablespoons butter

½ cup packed brown sugar

½ cup ketchup

¼ cup fresh lemon juice

½ teaspoon hot pepper sauce

½ teaspoon Worcestershire sauce

3 tablespoons finely minced sweet onions, like Vidalia

Melt butter in a small saucepan over medium-low heat. Whisk in brown sugar until sugar is dissolved. Whisk in ketchup, lemon juice, hot pepper and Worcestershire sauces, and onions. Reduce heat to low and cook, stirring occasionally, until thick, about 10 minutes. Serve immediately or transfer to a covered container and refrigerate until needed. To gently reheat sauce, place in a microwave-safe container and microwave for 30 seconds.

 Sauce will keep, refrigerated, for up to two weeks.　　　　**Makes:** 1 cup

Slow-Roasted Chipotle Pork Soft Tacos 🕐 4–8

Spicyyyyyyyy! This savory pork gets tamed when smothered with guacamole and sour cream in corn tortillas. These Mexican tacos are smokin' hot! You may want to add a bucket of cervezas (beer), like Corona or Dos Equis, to the serving sideboard to put out the chipotle fire.

3 tablespoons coarse salt

1 tablespoon chipotle chile pepper powder

1 (3- to 3½-pound) pork loin roast

24 small corn or flour tortillas

2 cups guacamole

2 cups sour cream

2 limes, cut into wedges

½ cup snipped fresh cilantro

Mix salt and chipotle powder together in a small bowl. Sprinkle mixture on all sides of pork roast, rubbing it into the surface of the meat. Place pork in a 5-quart slow cooker. Cook on low setting for 6 to 6½ hours, until pork shreds when tested with a fork. Transfer pork to a large platter and shred it, using 2 forks. Cover with aluminum foil.

Heat tortillas on a medium-hot griddle or in a large nonstick skillet over medium heat. Turn them frequently with tongs until they are heated through and soft. Stack tortillas and wrap them in a large cloth napkin. Place in a basket.

To serve: Remove foil from platter of pork. Place on table or serving sideboard along with basket of tortillas, plate of lime wedges, and bowls of guacamole, sour cream, and cilantro. Allow diners to assemble their own stuffed tortillas: Place 2 tortillas (one atop the other) on a dinner plate. Spread guacamole and sour cream over top tortilla. Place a portion of chipotle pork on tortilla. Squeeze lime juice over pork and sprinkle with cilantro. Fold double-tortilla in half before eating.

⏺ To make the pork ahead of time and freeze, mix a jar of mild salsa with the shredded pork to keep it moist. Freeze in a covered container for up to one month. To serve: Defrost pork and place it in a shallow baking dish covered with aluminum foil and reheat in a 325°F oven for 30 minutes. Continue with serving instructions above.

Serves: 4 (3 soft tacos each) or 6 (2 soft tacos each)

Shredded Pork and Sauerkraut Sammies

 4–8

Most of us have a love/hate affair with sauerkraut. My husband and I both grew up with the odors of baking pork and sauerkraut emanating from our German grandmothers' kitchens. He hated it! I loved it! I think the secret is that my grandmother thoroughly washed and drained the sauerkraut before cooking it with sugar.

1 tablespoon olive oil
1 (3- to 3-½ pound) pork loin roast
Salt and black pepper
1 cup chopped onions, like Vidalia
1 (32-ounce) bag sauerkraut,
    rinsed and drained

2 cups diced peeled apples
½ cup brown sugar
⅛ teaspoon ground cloves
12 sesame seed Kaiser rolls
¾ cup cranberry or cherry honey mustard
12 Swiss cheese slices

Place olive oil in a large nonstick skillet over medium heat. Season pork with salt and black pepper to taste. Sear all sides of pork in hot skillet until browned, about 3 minutes. Remove pork from skillet and set aside.

Place onions in skillet and sauté until softened, about 2 minutes. Transfer onions to a large bowl. Add sauerkraut, apples, brown sugar, ¼ teaspoon black pepper, and ground cloves to bowl. Toss to mix ingredients.

Place one-third of the sauerkraut mixture in the bottom of a 5-quart slow cooker. Place seared pork roast atop kraut mixture. Spread remaining two-thirds sauerkraut mixture over roast.

Cover and cook on low setting for 6 to 7 hours. Remove pork, shred meat, then mix with sauerkraut. Season with salt and pepper to taste.

To serve: Preheat oven to 325°F. Cut Kaiser buns in half across the middle, place on a baking sheet, and toast in oven. Spread ½ tablespoon mustard on the cut side of each bun. Place about ¾ cup shredded pork and sauerkraut mixture on bottom bun. Place 1 cheese slice atop pork. Replace top bun and cut sandwich in half.

Freeze leftover pork and sauerkraut in cupcake tins. Then pop out the frozen mixture and store in a zipper bag in the freezer. Defrost these single-portion servings when you get a hankering for a sandwich.

Serves: 12

Greek Pork Chops

Loaded with classic Greek ingredients, this piquant sauce transforms the everyday American pork chop into company fare. It is important to use very thick, bone-in chops in this recipe. Serve with Parmesan-topped rice or orzo.

2 (10- to 12-ounce) bone-in pork chops

Lemon-herb seasoning

1 teaspoon flour

1 tablespoon plus 1 teaspoon olive oil

2 cups halved and thinly sliced sweet onions, like Vidalia

½ cup golden raisins

1 tablespoon garlic paste or finely minced garlic

¾ cup quartered grape tomatoes

1 tablespoon sugar

1 teaspoon dried oregano leaves

¼ cup marsala wine

½ cup chicken broth

2 tablespoons white balsamic or white wine vinegar

¼ cup quartered pimento-stuffed green olives

1 tablespoon capers, rinsed and drained

2 tablespoons crumbled feta cheese, divided

Sprinkle both sides of pork chops with lemon-herb seasoning to taste. Place flour in a small sieve and sprinkle it on both sides of chops. Place 1 tablespoon olive oil in a large nonstick skillet over medium heat. Add chops and sauté for 1½ minutes per side, until browned. Transfer chops to a 2-quart slow cooker.

Add onions to skillet over medium heat and sauté, stirring frequently, for 1½ minutes. Add raisins and sauté for 30 seconds. Spread onions and raisins over pork chops. Add 1 teaspoon olive oil to skillet over medium heat. Add garlic and sauté for 30 seconds. Add tomatoes, sugar, and oregano, and sauté for 30 seconds, stirring constantly. Pour in wine, broth, and vinegar, and bring to a boil. Boil about 1 minute. Pour mixture over chops in slow cooker. Sprinkle with olives and capers.

Cover slow cooker and cook on low setting for 4 to 4 ½ hours, until chops are tender enough to be cut with a sharp knife, but are not shredding. (Chops should be the consistency of a grilled steak.)

To serve: Place 1 chop on each dinner plate. Sprinkle each with 1 tablespoon feta cheese. Top with a generous portion of sauce. Serve remaining sauce on the side.

To serve 4, double the recipe and use a 4- or 5-quart slow cooker. Cooking time will remain the same as long as total ingredients fill the slow cooker at least two-thirds full. If cooker is less than two-thirds full, reduce cooking time.

Serves: 2

Pork Chops and Onions in Gado Gado Sauce 4–8

Gado gado is a traditional Indonesian dish consisting of a vegetable salad topped with peanut sauce dressing. In this recipe, thick pork chops and sliced onions slowly simmer in a sweet, citrusy gado gado–style peanut sauce. If you'd like a little fire in your sauce add a couple of teaspoons of Asian sweet chili sauce.

⅓ cup creamy peanut butter

⅓ cup frozen orange juice concentrate, defrosted

⅓ cup honey

2 teaspoons garlic paste or finely minced garlic

2 teaspoons gingerroot paste or finely minced gingerroot

1 tablespoon soy sauce

2 teaspoons seasoned salt

4 bone-in pork chops, 1½ inches thick (about 2½ pounds)

1 tablespoon olive oil

3 cups halved, sliced sweet onions, like Vidalia

Mix peanut butter, orange juice concentrate, honey, garlic, gingerroot, and soy sauce together in a medium bowl. Set aside.

Sprinkle seasoned salt over both sides of each pork chop. Rub seasoned salt into chops. Place oil in a large nonstick skillet over medium heat. When oil is hot, add pork chops and sear each side, about 30 seconds per side. Remove chops from skillet and place on a dinner plate.

Place half the sliced onions in the bottom of a 4-quart slow cooker. Dip 2 pork chops into peanut sauce, liberally coating both sides. Place chops atop onions in slow cooker. Add remaining onions to slow cooker in an even layer. Dip remaining 2 pork chops into peanut sauce, liberally coating both sides. Place chops atop onions. Pour remaining sauce over pork chops and onions.

Cover slow cooker and cook on low setting for 6 to 7 hours, until chops are tender but not falling apart.

To serve: Serve chops topped with onions and drizzled with peanut sauce. Serve remaining sauce on the side.

I like to use Penzeys 4/S seasoned salt (www.penzeys.com). It is a mixture of sea salt, sugar, black pepper, paprika, onion, turmeric, and garlic. You can substitute your favorite seasoning blend.

Serves: 4

Russian Cherry Orchard Pork Stew

As witnessed in Chekhov's The Cherry Orchard, *Russians love cherries, which grow profusely in the country's central region. The pork simmers to fork-tenderness, absorbing the subtle sweetness of the cherries.*

¼ cup flour

1 tablespoon lemon-herb seasoning

2½ pounds pork loin roast, cut into 1-inch cubes

4 tablespoons butter, divided

1½ cups chopped onions, like Vidalia

2 (20-ounce) cans no-sugar-added cherry pie filling, divided

1 teaspoon salt

3 tablespoons lemon juice

⅛ teaspoon ground nutmeg

½ teaspoon crushed red pepper flakes

1 (16-ounce) can large butter beans, rinsed and drained

1½ to 2 teaspoons Kitchen Bouquet

Place flour and lemon-herb seasoning in a quart-size, freezer-weight zipper bag. Add pork pieces in batches, closing bag and shaking until pork is well coated with flour. Shake off excess flour and transfer floured pork to a dinner plate.

Place 2 tablespoons butter in a large nonstick skillet over medium heat. Add half the pork and cook until browned, 2 to 3 minutes. Transfer pork to a 4-quart slow cooker. Add remaining 2 tablespoons butter to skillet and brown remaining pork. Transfer pork to slow cooker. Sprinkle any remaining flour and seasoning over pork.

Add onions to skillet and sauté until onions have softened and browned slightly, about 3 minutes. Transfer to slow cooker. Add 1 can pie filling, salt, lemon juice, nutmeg, and red pepper flakes. Stir to combine ingredients. Top with remaining can of pie filling.

Cover slow cooker and cook on low setting for 4 hours. Add butter beans and stir to combine. Re-cover slow cooker and cook for 30 minutes. Stir in Kitchen Bouquet so that stew is a ruby-tinged bronze color. Serve in large shallow soup or pasta bowls.

The stew tastes even better if it is made a day ahead and flavors are allowed to marry overnight. To serve, reheat gently in a large saucepan on low heat. The recipe is equally tasty made with veal stew meat, if you can find it.

Serves: 4 to 6

Indochine Pineapple Pork Stew

 4–8

*At the same time sweet and spicy, this recipe showcases the flavors of Indochina —
pineapple, hot chiles, tomato, tamarind, coconut, and peanuts. Indochina is a region of
Southeast Asia, east of India and southwest of China. The name "Indochine" was coined
by French colonizers as a contraction of India and China.*

1 cup Coco Lopez Cream of Coconut	½ cup flour
½ cup pineapple juice	2 pounds pork loin roast, cut into 1-inch pieces
¼ cup tamarind syrup	Salt and freshly ground black pepper
¼ cup Asian sweet chili sauce	1 tablespoon olive oil
1 tablespoon Thai chili garlic paste	2 cups chopped onions
¼ cup teriyaki sauce	2 tablespoons garlic paste or finely minced garlic
2 tablespoons soy sauce	
2 tablespoon rice wine vinegar	2 cups (1-inch-dice) fresh pineapple
3 tablespoons honey	1 (14.5-ounce) can petite-diced tomatoes, drained
2 tablespoons peanut butter	

Up to 2 weeks ahead: Prepare Indochine sauce: Place cream of coconut, pineapple juice, tamarind syrup, and sweet chili sauce in a blender. Pulse until smooth. Add chili garlic paste, teriyaki and soy sauces, vinegar, and honey. Pulse until smooth. Add peanut butter and pulse until smooth. Transfer sauce to a covered container until needed. (Makes 3 cups.)

Place flour in a quart-size, freezer-weight zipper bag. Add pork pieces in batches, closing bag and shaking until pork is well coated with flour. Shake off excess flour and transfer floured pork to a dinner plate. Season with salt and pepper to taste.

Place oil in a large nonstick skillet over medium heat. Add pork in batches and cook until browned, 2 to 3 minutes. Transfer pork to a 4-quart slow cooker. Add onions and garlic to skillet. Sauté until onion has softened and browned slightly, about 2 minutes. Transfer to slow cooker.

Add pineapple, tomatoes, and 1 cup Indochine sauce to slow cooker. Stir to combine ingredients. Cover slow cooker and cook on low setting for 5 hours, until pork has cooked through and is tender when tested with the point of a knife.

To serve: Serve pork and sauce with Persian Rice (page 121).

The Indochine sauce also makes a wonderful marinade for beef, chicken, or shrimp. Used sparingly, the sauce is great drizzled over a vegetable salad. Tamarind syrup is made from the fruit of the tamarind tree. You can order it on Amazon.com. One bottle will last you a lifetime.

Serves: 4 to 6

Hoisin-Ginger Barbecued Baby Back Ribs ⏱ 4–8

A nice change from the tomato-based barbecue sauces usually served with ribs, this Asian-inspired sauce is light, sweet, and spicy. The method of first slow-cooking the ribs before grilling guarantees moist, juicy ribs every time. You can use any favorite barbecue sauce in this recipe.

Spice rub of choice

5 pounds baby back ribs (2 racks, each cut into thirds)

½ cup hoisin sauce

3 tablespoons rice vinegar

3 tablespoons soy sauce

1 tablespoon sesame oil

1 tablespoon finely minced crystallized ginger

2 teaspoons garlic paste or finely minced garlic

1 teaspoon Chinese five-spice powder

Liberally sprinkle your choice of spice rub over ribs. Rub into meat with clean hands. Place ribs in a 5- or 6-quart slow cooker and cook on low setting for 5 hours, until an inserted knife cuts through meat easily but meat is not falling off the bone. (You can hold ribs for up to 2 hours on warm setting.)

When ribs are almost done, place hoisin sauce, vinegar, soy sauce, sesame oil, ginger, garlic, and five-spice powder in a small nonstick saucepan over low heat. Cook for 8 minutes, stirring frequently, until sauce is thick and smooth. Remove from heat and transfer to a small bowl.

Preheat gas grill to 450 to 500°F. Place rib racks on grill, using indirect cooking method (see 🕐 below). Spread sauce over ribs. Grill for 10 minutes. Turn ribs over and grill for 2 minutes more. Turn ribs right side up, spread with sauce, and grill for 8 minutes more.

To serve: Cut into individual ribs and serve immediately with remaining sauce on the side.

🕐 To use the indirect grilling method, do not turn on burners under the meat being cooked. Instead, turn on burners on either side of meat and place an aluminum foil drip pan underneath meat, to collect fat and juices so that they do not burn.

Serves: 6 to 8

Mississippi Barbecued Country-Style Ribs ⏱ 4–8

My friend Kim Huffman, who attended Ole Miss, gave this recipe to me decades ago, swearing that it is the one and only authentic barbecue sauce in Mississippi. The lip-smacking good sauce is great with pulled pork, too, (page 72) but don't let a North Carolinian catch you saucing it that way! You'll need two slow cookers for this recipe.

4 to 5 pounds country-style pork ribs

Seasoning spice mix (see 🧄 below)

1 tablespoon butter

¾ cup chopped sweet onions, like Vidalia

1 (28-ounce) bottle Open Pit Barbecue Sauce (Original Flavor)

4 teaspoons Worcestershire sauce

2 teaspoons dry mustard

2 tablespoons brown sugar

⅓ cup ketchup

4 teaspoon white wine vinegar

Garlic powder

Lemon-pepper seasoning

Sprinkle seasoning spice mix liberally on all sides of each rib. Place ribs in a 5-quart slow cooker. Cover and cook on low setting for 5 hours, or until ribs are tender when poked with a fork but not falling off the bone. (Can hold ribs in slow cooker for up to 2 hours on warm setting.)

Meanwhile, melt butter in a medium nonstick skillet over medium heat. Add onions and sauté, stirring frequently, until soft, about 3 minutes. Transfer onions to a medium bowl. Add barbecue sauce, Worcestershire sauce, dry mustard, brown sugar, ketchup, and vinegar. Stir to combine. Add garlic powder and lemon-pepper seasoning to taste. Transfer sauce mixture to a 1½-quart slow cooker. Cover and cook on low setting for 4 hours, until sauce is thick and flavors have married. (Can hold sauce in slow cooker on warm setting for 2 to 2½ hours.)

To serve: Preheat a gas grill to medium-hot, about 450°F. Remove ribs from slow cooker and place on a platter. Brush each with barbecue sauce from small slow cooker. Place ribs on grill, sauced-side down, and cook for 6 minutes. Baste tops of ribs and turn them over, sauced-side down. Cook ribs for 6 minutes more.

To serve: Serve ribs with heated barbecue sauce on the side.

🧄 I use Lindberg-Snider Porterhouse & Roast Seasoning, which I found at my local butcher shop. It is a flavorful mixture of salt, granulated garlic, granulated onion, black pepper, oregano, paprika, celery seed, parsley, and rosemary. You can order it online at www.lindbergsnider.com or substitute your favorite spice rub.

Serves: 4

Honey-Baked Ham with Cumberland Sauce 4–8

You'll never buy honey-baked ham from the deli again. The slow cooking in honey and apple juice creates a juicy, full-flavored ham that will feed a crowd. Cumberland sauce was named after the Duke of Cumberland in the late nineteenth century. Even today it is the favored sauce to serve with ham, lamb, or venison in British households. Save the ham bone to make "Puy" Lentil Soup (page 15).

1 (8-pound) bone-in hickory-smoked half-ham	2 tablespoons fresh lime juice
¼ cup plus 2 tablespoons honey, divided	¼ cup pomegranate juice
¾ teaspoon ground cloves	1 tablespoon cornstarch
2 cups apple juice	¼ cup plus 2 tablespoons Dijon mustard
¾ cup red currant jelly	¼ cup plus 2 tablespoons maple syrup
¼ cup orange juice	¼ cup plus 2 tablespoons packed
2 tablespoons fresh lemon juice	dark brown sugar

Place ham in a 6-quart slow cooker, cut-side down. Drizzle ¼ cup honey all over ham. Sprinkle ground cloves over ham. Pour apple juice over ham. Cover and cook on low setting for 8 hours.

Meanwhile, to make Cumberland sauce, place jelly, citrus and pomegranate juices, and 2 tablespoons honey in a medium nonstick saucepan over medium heat. Bring to boil, then reduce heat to low. Place cornstarch in a small bowl. Whisk 2 tablespoons of the hot sauce mixture into cornstarch until smooth. Pour cornstarch mixture into saucepan and cook, whisking frequently, until sauce has thickened slightly. Serve immediately or transfer to a covered container and refrigerate until needed. Warm up sauce in a medium nonstick saucepan on low heat before serving. (Makes 1¾ cups.)

To serve: Place mustard, maple syrup, and brown sugar in a small saucepan over low heat. Cook, stirring frequently, until sugar has melted and sauce thickens slightly. Transfer ham to a cutting board. (Discard cooking juices.) Slice ham into ½-inch slices. Drizzle mustard–brown sugar sauce over ham slices. Serve with Cumberland sauce on the side.

If you use a pre-sliced ham, place the entire ham on a serving platter and drizzle some of the mustard-brown sugar sauce between the slices. The Cumberland sauce will thicken when reheated, so if you make it ahead, don't allow it to initially thicken too much. If the sauce does get too thick, thin it with a little orange or pomegranate juice.

Serves: 16

Brats 'n' Beer

-4

Simmering the bratwurst slowly in beer and onions cooks the sausages from the inside out, which keeps them juicy when finished on a hot grill. Placing them back in the simmering brew guarantees the brats stay moist until they are devoured.

12 bratwursts

2 (12-ounce) cans beer

4 cups sliced onions

Ketchup (optional)

Dijon or yellow mustard (optional)

Sauerkraut (optional)

Chopped onions (optional)

Place bratwursts, beer, and onions in a 5- or 6-quart slow cooker. Cook on low setting for 2 hours. Remove bratwurst from slow cooker with tongs. (Do not puncture skin or filling will ooze out.) Reduce heat setting to warm.

Preheat a gas grill. Cook bratwurst on a hot grill for 3 minutes on each side, turning carefully with tongs, until browned. Place grilled bratwurst back in the slow cooker until serving, up to 4 hours.

To serve: Serve brats on toasted buns, with condiments of your choice.

If you live in 'wurst country, you'll have plenty of bratwurst varieties from which to choose. In the rest of the U.S., look for Johnsonville Original or Johnsonville Beer 'n Bratwurst, which most closely look and taste like those you'd get from a 'wurst-country butcher.

Serves: 6 to 8

Lemon Chardonnay Chicken Florentine 4–8

Chicken Florentine made with spinach most likely originated in Renaissance France, where the Medici found it fashionable to hire Tuscan cooks who named their creations after their native country. Chicken Florentine made in Florence, Italy, however, uses artichokes instead of spinach.

2½ pounds skinless, boneless chicken breasts (about 4 large), quartered

2 teaspoons Fox Point Seasoning (see 🕑 below)

3 tablespoons fresh lemon juice

2 tablespoons capers with juice

¾ cup chicken broth

¼ cup chardonnay wine

2 tablespoons cornstarch

1 tablespoon olive oil

3 (1-pound) packages fresh baby spinach, washed and spun dry

½ cup shredded mozzarella

Season both sides of chicken breasts with the Fox Point blend. Place chicken in a 2-quart slow cooker.

Place lemon juice, capers, chicken broth, and chardonnay in a medium saucepan over medium heat. Bring to a boil. Transfer sauce to slow cooker. Stir to combine sauce with chicken. Cook on low setting for 3½ hours. Remove chicken to a dinner plate. Place cornstarch in a small bowl. Whisk in ¼ cup sauce from slow cooker. Whisk cornstarch mixture into sauce in slow cooker. Return chicken to slow cooker. Re-cover slow cooker and cook for 1 hour more. Reduce heat to warm setting.

To serve: Place oil in a large nonstick skillet over medium heat. Add a third of the spinach to skillet and sauté until barely wilted, about 1 minute, stirring constantly. Remove spinach with a slotted spoon and divide among 2 dinner plates. Repeat process twice more with remaining spinach. Top each of the 6 portions of spinach with 2 to 3 pieces of chicken. Drizzle each portion with lemon-chardonnay sauce. Sprinkle each serving with shredded mozzarella. Serve immediately.

🕑 Fox Point Seasoning is a great blend offered by Penzeys Spice Company (www.penzeys.com). It is a combination of salt, dried shallots, dried chives, garlic powder, onion powder, and ground green peppercorns. You can make up your own blend of these spices if you don't want to order the Fox Point. Or substitute your favorite spice blend instead.

Serves: 6

Sun-Dried Tomato and Mushroom-Sauced Chicken

Before modern food preservation methods, Italians dried the summer's bounty of tomatoes on their rooftop tiles for use during the winter months. It takes twenty pounds of tomatoes to produce one pound of sun-dried tomatoes.

2½ pounds skinless, boneless chicken breasts (about 4 large), cut into ½-inch slices

1 teaspoon salt

½ teaspoon black pepper

3 tablespoons butter

2 pounds white button mushroom caps, wiped clean and thinly sliced

⅔ cup minced shallots

½ cup slivered sun-dried tomatoes

2 tablespoons flour

¾ cup chicken broth

¼ cup dry white wine

3 tablespoons snipped fresh parsley

Place chicken breast slices in a 4-quart slow cooker. Sprinkle with salt and pepper and toss to combine.

Melt butter in a large nonstick skillet over medium heat. Add mushrooms, shallots, and sun-dried tomatoes. Sauté, stirring frequently, for 5 minutes, until mushrooms are soft and have released their liquid. Stir in flour. Slowly stir in broth and wine. Transfer mushroom mixture to slow cooker. Toss with chicken until well combined.

Cover slow cooker and cook on low setting for 3 hours. Stir chicken, re-cover, and cook for 1 hour more.

To serve: Serve this saucy chicken over orzo, penne, or mini raviolis. Sprinkle each serving with ½ tablespoon fresh parsley.

🕐 Do not use oil-packed sun-dried tomatoes in this recipe. Use the plain sun-dried tomatoes you'll find packaged in the produce section of your supermarket.

Serves: 6

Herbed Chicken Dijon

 4–8

Company fare straight from the slow cooker, this finely seasoned French chicken dish comes together in a flash. You can hold the chicken on warm setting for up to 1 hour.

½ cup flour

4 large skinless, boneless chicken breasts (about 2 pounds), cut in half

2 tablespoons olive oil

1 tablespoon gingerroot paste or peeled, minced gingerroot

2 teaspoons garlic paste or minced garlic

1 tablespoon Dijon mustard

1 teaspoon salt

1 teaspoon freshly ground black pepper

2 large plum tomatoes (about 9 ounces), thinly sliced

1 teaspoon snipped fresh flat-leaf parsley

1 teaspoon snipped fresh rosemary

¼ cup fresh bread crumbs

1 tablespoon butter, melted

Place flour in a large zipper bag. Add half the chicken pieces to bag. Close and shake bag until chicken is coated with flour. Shake off excess flour and transfer chicken to a dinner plate. Repeat with remaining chicken.

Place oil in a large nonstick skillet over medium heat. When oil is hot, add chicken. Sear chicken for about 30 seconds per side. Transfer chicken to a 2-quart slow cooker in a single, tight layer.

Mix gingerroot, garlic, and mustard together in a small bowl. Spread mustard paste over chicken. Sprinkle with salt and pepper. Place tomato slices in an even layer atop chicken. Sprinkle with parsley, rosemary, and bread crumbs. Drizzle melted butter over bread crumbs. Cover slow cooker and cook on low setting for 4 hours, until chicken is no longer pink when tested with a knife. (Chicken should just be cooked through and still moist.)

To serve: Remove each chicken breast from slow cooker, being careful to keep tomato slices and bread crumb mixture atop chicken. Place each serving on an individual dinner plate. Drizzle with cooking juices.

You can assemble all the ingredients in the slow cooker early in the day. Cover slow cooker insert with plastic wrap, and refrigerate until 4½ hours before serving. If chicken comes directly from refrigerator, you'll need to cook it an extra 30 minutes.

Serves: 6

Island Citrus Chicken

-4

Sweet and tangy, this citrusy sauce dresses up the common backyard chickens often seen roaming the islands of the Caribbean.

....

1⅓ to 1½ pounds skinless, boneless chicken breasts
3 tablespoons flour
½ cup orange marmalade
½ cup bottled shrimp cocktail sauce
2 teaspoons dry mustard
¼ teaspoon curry powder

....

Wash chicken and pat dry with paper toweling. Place flour on a dinner plate and dredge both sides of chicken breasts in flour. Transfer floured chicken breasts to a 2-quart slow cooker.

Mix marmalade, cocktail sauce, dry mustard, and curry powder together in a medium bowl. Pour sauce over chicken. Cover slow cooker and cook on low setting for 3 hours or until chicken is cooked through but not dry. (You can hold chicken on warm setting for up to 30 minutes.)

To serve: Slice chicken breasts in thin slices across the grain. Transfer to a serving platter. Drizzle sauce over chicken and serve immediately.

....

If you don't have bottled cocktail sauce, make your own by adding 1 tablespoon prepared horseradish (or to taste) to ½ cup ketchup.

Serves: 4

Chicken Marengo

 4–8

As the story goes, Napoleon Bonaparte successfully ended his Italian campaign with a victory over Austria in the Battle of Marengo, in Piedmont, Italy, on June 14, 1800. Securing ingredients from local farmers, his personal chef created the original version of this chicken dish for Napoleon's dinner that evening, cooking it while still in the battlefield. Napoleon so loved the dish, he had it prepared after every successful battle.

8 ounces hot pork sausage
½ cup flour
Salt and black pepper
1 teaspoon dried tarragon
3 pounds skinless, boneless chicken breasts (6), rinsed and patted dry with paper toweling
4 tablespoons butter, divided
8 ounces button mushrooms, wiped clean and sliced
1 teaspoon garlic paste or finely minced garlic
½ cup white wine
2 (14.5-ounce) cans diced tomatoes with basil, garlic, and oregano, drained with juices reserved
¼ teaspoon onion powder
1 pound pennette (miniature penne pasta)

Crumble sausage into a large nonstick saucepan over medium heat. Cook sausage, stirring frequently, until browned and cooked through. Transfer sausage to a 5½- to 6- quart slow cooker with a slotted spoon.

Mix flour, 1 teaspoon salt, ½ teaspoon pepper, and tarragon together on a dinner plate. Dredge chicken breasts in flour mixture, coating all sides. Reserve excess flour mixture.

Melt 2 tablespoons butter in skillet. Place half the floured chicken breasts in skillet, and sauté over medium heat until browned, about 1½ minutes per side. Transfer to slow cooker. Repeat process with remaining chicken breasts.

Add remaining 2 tablespoons butter to skillet. When butter has melted, add mushrooms and garlic, and sauté for 2 to 3 minutes. Reduce heat to low. Stir in remaining flour mixture. Add wine and ½ cup reserved juice from diced tomatoes. Stir until pan is deglazed and sauce has thickened, about 30 seconds. Stir in tomatoes and onion powder. Spoon mushroom-tomato mixture over chicken breasts and sausage.

Cover and cook on low setting for 4 hours until chicken is cooked through but not shredding. Adjust seasoning with salt and pepper to taste.

Bring a large pot of water to boil over high heat. Add pennette, reduce heat to medium, and cook according to manufacturer's instructions until pasta is al dente, about 8 minutes. Drain pasta in a colander.

To serve: Place a portion of pasta and 1 chicken breast on each dinner plate. Spoon sauce over chicken and pasta and serve immediately.

⊙ If you'd like sliced onions in this dish, sauté them with the mushrooms and eliminate the onion powder.

Serves: 6

Chicken and Sweet Potato Stew

 4–8

My two trips to Africa revealed unexpectedly interesting cuisine — complex flavors concocted from ingredients that can also be commonly found in United States, such as sweet potatoes, hot chilies, and peanuts.

2 pounds skinless, boneless chicken breasts, cut into 1½-inch chunks

Salt and freshly ground black pepper

1 cup chopped sweet onions, like Vidalia

2 large sweet potatoes, peeled, sliced 1¼ inches thick, and slices quartered

2 to 3 fresh serrano chilies, thinly sliced (see ⊖ below)

3 large tomatoes, peeled and cut into large dice

½ teaspoon coarse salt

½ teaspoon sugar

½ cup chunky peanut butter

½ cup hot water

3 teaspoons garlic paste or finely minced garlic

½ cup red currant jelly

Liberally season chicken with salt and pepper. Place chicken in a 5-quart slow cooker. Add onions, sweet potatoes, chilies, and tomatoes. Stir so that ingredients are well mixed. Sprinkle ingredients with coarse salt and sugar.

Place peanut butter in a medium bowl. Whisk in water and garlic paste. Pour mixture over ingredients in slow cooker. Cook on low setting for 5 hours. Stir in red currant jelly. Re-cover and cook for 30 minutes more on low setting, or reduce heat to warm and hold for 1 hour.

To serve: Serve in large, shallow soup bowls.

⊖ I use 3 serrano chilies in this recipe, which makes the dish very spicy. If you prefer less heat, use only 1 or 2 chilies. To easily peel tomatoes, bring a medium saucepan of water to a boil over high heat. Cut an X on top and stem ends of tomatoes. Add tomatoes to boiling water, one at a time, leaving them in the water for only about 15 seconds. Remove tomatoes to a work surface with tongs. Use a paring knife to slip skins off tomatoes.

Serves: 6

Med-Rim Chicken

 4–8

The cuisines of countries rimming the Mediterranean Sea offer a wide variety of different flavor combinations. This dish is reminiscent of something you might enjoy in Spain, Portugal, or Greece. Serve the chicken atop a bed of steamed rice or al dente pasta of choice, topped with the piquant sauce.

1 (4-pound) chicken, cut in pieces
2 to 3 teaspoons Greek seasoning blend (see ⊙ below)
2 tablespoons canola oil
2 cups chopped sweet onions, like Vidalia
1 tablespoon capers, rinsed and drained
½ cup small pimento-stuffed olives, cut in half
½ cup golden raisins

4 teaspoons garlic paste or finely minced garlic
2 tablespoons lemon juice
½ teaspoon ground cumin
1 teaspoon dried oregano
½ teaspoon caper juice
¼ cup dry white wine
¼ cup firmly packed brown sugar
Salt and freshly ground black pepper

Wash chicken, pat dry with paper toweling, and cut off excess skin and fat. Sprinkle seasoning blend over both sides of each chicken piece. Place oil in a large nonstick skillet over medium heat. Place chicken, skin-sides down, in skillet. Cook for 2 minutes per side, until golden brown. Transfer chicken to a 4- or 5-quart slow cooker.

Top chicken with onions, capers, olives, and raisins. Place garlic, lemon juice, cumin, oregano, caper juice, and white wine in a small bowl. Whisk until smooth. Pour mixture over chicken. Sprinkle brown sugar over chicken.

Cook on low setting for 5 hours or until chicken is tender. Season with salt and pepper to taste before serving.

⊙ I use a Greek seasoning blend from Penzey's Spice Company (www.penzeys.com) but you can make your own. Mix together 1½ teaspoons dried oregano, ½ teaspoon garlic powder, 1 teaspoon dried lemon peel, ½ teaspoon dried marjoram, ½ teaspoon black pepper, ½ teaspoon salt, ½ teaspoon onion powder. Store in an airtight container.

Serves: 4

Jamaican Jerk Chicken

-4

Jerking is a method of seasoning and cooking meat that dates back to the Carib-Arawak Indians who inhabited Jamaica. Meat is marinated in a spicy pastelike sauce and then cooked slowly. Originally cooks would puncture the meat with a sharp object and stuff the holes with a variety of spices. The meat would then be cooked in a deep pit lined with stones over burning pimento (allspice) wood, which gave it a unique smoky flavor.

1 cup chopped sweet onions, like Vidalia

⅓ cup chopped scallions

1 teaspoon dried thyme or 2 teaspoons fresh thyme

1 teaspoon salt

1 teaspoon black pepper

2 teaspoons sugar

1 teaspoon ground allspice

½ teaspoon ground nutmeg

½ teaspoon ground cinnamon

2 whole jalapeño peppers, sliced

3 tablespoons soy sauce

1 tablespoon canola oil

1 tablespoon cider vinegar

4 pounds cut-up chicken pieces, skin removed

One day ahead: Place all ingredients except chicken in the bowl of a food processor. Puree, scraping down the sides of the bowl several times, until mixture is smooth. Place chicken in a large freezer-weight zipper bag. Pour marinade mixture into bag. Close bag and massage chicken so that all pieces are well coated with marinade. Refrigerate chicken in bag overnight.

To cook: Remove chicken from marinade and place in a 4-quart slow cooker. Discard marinade. Cook on low setting for 3½ hours, until chicken has cooked through but is not falling off the bone.

Preheat a gas grill to medium-hot, about 450°F. Sear chicken for 2½ minutes per side.

To serve: Serve with steamed white rice or boiled fingerling potatoes.

Jerk chicken usually calls for Scotch bonnet pepper, or the similar habanero. These are the hottest peppers in the capsicum family. I have lightened the spice in this recipe by using jalapeños, which are much milder. If you want to authenticate this recipe and love hot, hot, hot, substitute one scotch bonnet pepper for the jalapeños.

Serves: 4 to 6

Fruited Chicken

Called mancha manteles *or "tablecloth stainers" in Mexico, this fruit-laden stew is spiked with cinnamon and chili powder. Serve with steamed white rice or Persian Rice (page 121).*

2 tablespoons olive oil

4½ pounds skinless, boneless chicken thighs, excess fat trimmed

1 cup chopped sweet onions, like Vidalia

1 cup diced green bell peppers

¼ cup slivered almonds

½ cup crushed tomatoes or tomato puree

1 (15-ounce) can mandarin orange segments, drained with juices reserved

2 teaspoons chili powder

1 teaspoon salt

½ teaspoon ground cinnamon

1 tablespoon Gourmet Garden Mexican Herb and Spice Blend paste

2 sweet-tart apples, peeled, cored, and sliced

2 bananas, peeled and sliced into ½-inch pieces

2 tablespoons cornstarch

Place oil in a large nonstick skillet over medium heat. Working in 2 batches, brown chicken on both sides, about 1 minute total. Transfer to a 5- or 6-quart slow cooker. Add onions, bell peppers, and almonds to skillet. Sauté until vegetables are browned slightly, about 3 minutes.

Transfer vegetables to a blender. Add tomato puree, ½ cup reserved mandarin orange juice, chili powder, salt, cinnamon, and Mexican spice blend. Puree until smooth.

Pour mixture over chicken in slow cooker. Cover slow cooker and cook on low setting for 3 hours. Add apples, bananas, and reserved mandarin oranges. Re-cover slow cooker and cook for 1½ hours more, until apples have cooked through but are not mushy.

To serve: Remove chicken and fruit with a slotted spoon and place in a low-sided serving dish (fruit on top of chicken). Cover with aluminum foil. Place cornstarch in a medium bowl. Whisk in 1 cup of sauce from slow cooker until smooth. Whisk cornstarch mixture into slow cooker. Cover slow cooker and cook over high setting for 5 to 10 minutes, whisking occasionally, until sauce has thickened. Pour sauce over fruit and chicken and serve immediately.

You can substitute chunked canned pineapple for the mandarin oranges and juice. Gourmet Garden Mexican Herb and Spice Blend paste is sold in the produce section of your supermarket. It is a tasty combination of herbs and spices traditionally found in Mexican cuisine.

Serves: 8

Lebanese Orange-Apricot Chicken -4

The Med Rim is Europe's best source of fresh and dried fruits as well as the world's olive provider. This dish defies national borders. You could find a similar dish in Israel, Turkey, and other countries of the Med Rim region. Serve the dish with the Lebanese anise-flavored liquor, arak. Usually served in a small glass, arak, which is a clear liquid, is mixed with several tablespoons water, which turns it milky. Watch out though. The drinks go down smoothly but deliver quite a wallop!

2 pounds skinless, boneless chicken thighs, cut into 1-inch chunks

5 large cloves garlic, peeled and crushed

1 cup chopped dried apricots

½ cup chopped pitted Greek black olives

1 tablespoon grated fresh orange peel

1 orange, peeled, segmented, and chopped, with juices

¼ cup apricot preserves

3 tablespoons orange juice

1 tablespoon lemon juice

2 tablespoons snipped fresh fennel leaves

1 tablespoon finely minced fennel

½ cup light brown sugar

Place chicken, garlic, apricots, olives, orange peel, orange segments with juice, apricot preserves, orange juice, lemon juice, snipped fennel leaves, and minced fennel in a large bowl. Toss ingredients until well mixed.

Transfer to a 4-quart slow cooker. Sprinkle brown sugar over chicken mixture. Cover and cook on low setting for 3 hours, until chicken is cooked through but not dried out.

To serve: Serve with steamed white rice.

You'll find fresh fennel in the produce section of your supermarket. Fennel is a greenish-white bulb that is sold with its stems and feathery leaves attached. The leaves resemble fresh dill. The fennel bulb has a delicate licorice flavor and is great slivered and added to tossed salad. Serve this dish with orzo or rice.

Serves: 4 to 6

Chinese Roast Chicken

 4–8

Artist/culinary expert Carol Mann shares this Asian-spiced chicken recipe designed especially for the slow cooker. Placing the bird breast down ensures the juices run into the meat and not into the slow cooker.

1 (4- to 5-pound) roasting chicken, like Perdue Oven Stuffer
1 stalk celery, cut into 2-inch lengths
6 sprigs fresh curly parsley
2 (2-inch) pieces peeled gingerroot
2 scallions, cut into 2-inch lengths
1 tablespoon soy sauce
1 teaspoon Chinese five-spice powder
1 teaspoon gingerroot paste or finely minced gingerroot

Remove neck and giblets from chicken cavity and discard. Rinse chicken and pat dry with paper toweling. Stuff cavity with celery, parsley, gingerroot pieces, and scallions. Tie chicken legs together with kitchen twine.

Mix soy sauce, five-spice powder, and gingerroot paste together in a small bowl. Using a small spoon, spread spice paste over breast side of chicken. Place a rack in the bottom of a 5- or 6-quart slow cooker (see 🕐 below). Place chicken on rack, breast down. Spread spice paste over back of chicken.

Cover slow cooker and cook for 5 hours, until leg separates from body when pulled and juices run clear when breast meat is tested with a knife.

To serve: Discard vegetables from chicken cavity. Slice chicken and serve.

🕐 It is important to cook the chicken on a rack so that it does not swim in its own juices and end up stewing. Most slow cookers do not come with a rack insert. I created my own rack by rolling aluminum foil into logs about 4 inches long and 2 inches thick. Three foil logs placed crosswise in slow cooker, equal distance apart, make an adequate rack for cooking the chicken.

Serves: 4

Turkey Breast with Orange-Cranberry Sauce 4–8

Succulent turkey enveloped in tart cranberry sauce combines two of the best dishes of a Thanksgiving feast . . . any time of the year.

1 (3-pound) boneless turkey breast roast, such as Butterball

2 cups fresh cranberries, picked over and rinsed

2 tablespoons sugar

⅓ cup orange juice concentrate

1 tablespoon grated orange peel

½ cup chicken broth

Place turkey breast in a 4-quart slow cooker. Place cranberries in a medium nonstick saucepan over medium heat. Sprinkle with sugar. Add orange juice concentrate, orange peel, and chicken broth. Stir to combine. Cook, stirring occasionally, until cranberries pop and mixture comes to a boil, 4 to 5 minutes.

Pour cranberry mixture over turkey breast. Cover slow cooker and cook on low setting for 6 hours.

To serve: Transfer turkey breast to a cutting board and cut into ½-inch slices. Transfer orange-cranberry sauce to a serving bowl. Ladle orange-cranberry sauce over each serving of turkey.

This orange-cranberry sauce is thin, like an au jus. If you'd like a thicker sauce, transfer sauce to a medium nonstick saucepan over medium heat. Whisk together 1 tablespoon cornstarch and 1 tablespoon of the sauce in a small bowl. Whisk cornstarch mixture into sauce. Cook, stirring constantly, until sauce thickens, 2 to 3 minutes.

Serves: 4 to 6

Stuffed or Layered Specialties

- Picadillo-Stuffed Sweet Onions – *Cuba*
- Stuffed Grape Leaves with Lemon Sauce – *Med Rim/Middle East*
- Stuffed Bell Peppers – *Middle East*
- Chicken and Sausage Manicotti – *Italy*
- Mexicana Lasagna – *Mexico/Italy Fusion*
- Moussaka – *Greece*
- Mac 'n' Cheese with Caramelized Onions and Tomatoes – *USA*

Picadillo-Stuffed Sweet Onions

 4–8

Picadillo (pronounced peek-a-dee-yo) is one of the most popular dishes in Cuban cuisine. Usually family fare served with fried plantains and black beans, picadillo achieves dinner party status when stuffed into sweet onions and slow-cooked to perfection. You can prepare the picadillo and stuff the onions a day ahead of time, and pop them into the slow cooker hours before your guests arrive.

4 large sweet onions, like Vidalia, peeled

2 teaspoons olive oil

2 teaspoons garlic paste or finely minced garlic

1 pound ground beef

1 tablespoon Grand Marnier liqueur (optional)

½ cup raisins

⅓ cup sliced pimento-stuffed green olives

2 tablespoons capers, rinsed and drained

⅓ cup tomato paste

½ teaspoon ground cumin

¼ teaspoon dried oregano

¾ teaspoon salt

¼ teaspoon black pepper

1 cup beef broth

2 tablespoons butter, melted

Slice off the stem end of each onion (about ½ inch from stem). Using a serrated melon ball scoop, remove the interior of each onion, leaving the outer 2 layers intact and forming an onion bowl. Place a piece of onion over the hole in the bottom of each onion so the stuffing can't escape. Set onion bowls aside. Chop scooped onions into medium dice. Reserve 2 cups for use in this recipe. Place remaining chopped onions in a zipper bag and refrigerate for future use.

Place oil in a large nonstick skillet over medium heat. Add reserved 2 cups chopped onions and sauté, stirring occasionally, for 2½ minutes. Add garlic and sauté for 30 seconds. Add ground beef and cook, stirring frequently until meat is browned, about 7 minutes. Drain beef mixture in a colander. Wipe out skillet with paper toweling and return meat mixture to skillet.

Place skillet over medium heat. Add liqueur, raisins, olives, capers, tomato paste, cumin, oregano, salt, and pepper. Stir to combine ingredients. Cover skillet and cook meat mixture, stirring occasionally, for 7 minutes, until flavors marry. Pour beef broth into a 6-quart slow cooker (or any size that will accommodate the 4 onions). Brush interior cavity and outer surfaces of each onion with melted butter. Spoon picadillo mixture into each onion, forming a mound on top. Stand onions upright in slow cooker. Cover and cook on low setting for 4 hours, until onions have cooked through. (You can hold the stuffed onions on warm setting for up to 30 minutes.)

If you have any picadillo left over after stuffing the onions, you can serve it the next day for lunch in 3-inch slider buns, like a Sloppy Joe.

Serves: 4

Stuffed Grape Leaves with Lemon Sauce 4–8

Nearly every country in the Med Rim and the Middle East serves a variation of stuffed grape leaves. In this Greek version, called dolmades, *a savory mixture of ground lamb, rice, and mint is stuffed into the leaves.*

1 tablespoon olive oil
2 cups chopped sweet onions, like Vidalia
2 teaspoons salt, divided
1 pound ground lamb
½ cup uncooked jasmine or other long-grain rice
¼ teaspoon black pepper
2 tablespoons snipped fresh mint
1 (15.2-ounce) jar grape leaves
1½ cups water
¾ cup dry white wine
¾ cup chicken broth
¼ cup fresh lemon juice
2 teaspoons cornstarch
1½ teaspoons sugar
2 tablespoons butter

Place oil in a large nonstick skillet over medium heat. Add onions and 1 teaspoon salt. Sauté onions until soft but not brown, about 4 minutes, stirring occasionally. Transfer half the onions to a large bowl. Add lamb, rice, pepper, 1 teaspoon salt, and mint to bowl. Mix ingredients together with clean hands.

Rinse grape leaves and drain on paper toweling. Carefully separate leaves. Place a double layer of leaves on a clean work surface. Place a rounded measuring tablespoon of the lamb mixture in the middle of the leaves. Fold stem ends over lamb filling, then fold in the sides and roll leaves up tightly. Place rolled leaves, seam-side down, in the bottom of a 2-quart slow cooker. Repeat process with remaining leaves and meat filling, creating 2 layers of stuffed, rolled leaves.

Sprinkle remaining onions over rolled grape leaves. Pour 1½ cups water over contents in slow cooker. Cover slow cooker and cook on low setting for 4 to 4½ hours, until rice and lamb are cooked through and leaves are tender.

About 30 minutes before serving, make lemon sauce: Place wine and broth in a 2-quart nonstick saucepan over medium-high heat. Bring to a boil and cook about 8 minutes, stirring frequently, until mixture reduces by half (about ¾ cup). Whisk together lemon juice, cornstarch, and sugar in a small bowl, then slowly stir it into broth mixture. Keep stirring until sauce boils again. Stir in butter. Reduce heat to low, cover saucepan, and keep sauce warm.

To serve: Using a slotted spoon, transfer stuffed grape leaves to a serving platter. Drizzle with lemon sauce. Serve remaining sauce on the side.

You'll find jars of grape leaves in the international section of your supermarket or specialty grocery.

Serves: 8

Stuffed Bell Peppers

 4–8

Just about every cuisine in the world has a version of stuffed bell peppers This recipe spotlights the seasonings of ancient Persia, which used copious amounts of parsley and mint as well as a concoction of spices known as advieh (see ⬤ opposite).

¼ cup basmati or long-grain rice

¼ cup yellow split peas

2 cups water

8 red, yellow, and/or orange bell peppers

1 tablespoon olive oil

1 cup chopped sweet onions, like Vidalia

1 pound ground beef

2 tablespoons tomato paste

1 cup snipped fresh flat-leaf parsley

½ cup snipped fresh mint

½ cup minced scallions

1 teaspoon dried tarragon

2¼ teaspoons salt, divided

½ teaspoon black pepper

¼ teaspoon advieh (see ⬤ opposite)

1½ cups tomato juice

¼ cup light brown sugar

1 tablespoon fresh lemon juice

Place rice and split peas in a medium bowl. Add water to cover, then agitate with your hand. Drain off water. Repeat process two more times to remove excess starch from rice. Drain mixture in a colander. Place rinsed rice and peas and 2 cups water in a medium saucepan over high heat. Bring to a boil, stir, and reduce heat to medium. Cook for 15 minutes, stirring occasionally. Transfer mixture to a colander. Rinse and drain.

Meanwhile, cut tops off bell peppers. Remove seeds and ribs from interior of peppers. Rinse and drain on paper toweling.

Place olive oil in a large nonstick skillet over medium heat. Add onions and ground beef and cook, stirring frequently, until meat is browned, about 5 minutes. Stir in tomato paste. Remove from heat and stir in rice and split peas.

Transfer meat mixture to a large bowl. Add parsley, mint, scallions, tarragon, 1 teaspoon salt, black pepper, and advieh. Toss until ingredients are well combined.

Coat the interior of a 6-quart slow cooker with vegetable cooking spray. Fill each bell pepper with meat stuffing and place upright in slow cooker.

Whisk tomato juice, brown sugar, lemon juice, and ¼ teaspoon salt together in a measuring cup. Pour liquid around stuffed peppers in slow cooker, taking care not to pour liquid into the stuffing.

Cover slow cooker and cook on low setting for 5 to 6 hours, until peppers are soft. Transfer peppers to a serving platter.

To serve: Drizzle sauce from slow cooker over peppers. Serve immediately, 2 peppers per person.

. . . .

Advieh is a Persian rice seasoning composed of many spices. You can find it at a Middle Eastern market or online at: www.sadaf.com. To make a reasonable facsimile on your own, mix together 1 teaspoon ground cinnamon, 1 teaspoon ground nutmeg, 1 teaspoon ground cardamom, and ½ teaspoon ground cumin. Store in an airtight container. (Authentic advieh also contains ground rose petals, not readily found in an American supermarket. If you do find it, add 1 teaspoon to your advieh mixture, but the seasoning will be fine without it.)

If you can't find yellow split peas, use all rice instead. Yellow, red, and orange peppers are sweeter than green peppers, which are not yet ripe. Chop up the tops of peppers and reserve for use in a tossed salad.

Serves: 4

. . . .

Chicken and Sausage Manicotti

⏱ 4–8

These baked stuffed pasta tubes couldn't be easier to prepare. You can make up the filling in advance and freeze it until needed. A batch of Real Deal Italian Meatless Sauce (page 30) makes 6 cups and freezes well. And best of all, you don't have to boil the dried pasta before assembling the manicotti. Simply stuff the dried tubes, place in the slow cooker covered with sauce, and walk away!

4 ounces skinless, boneless chicken breast, cut into ½-inch dice

4 ounces spicy pork sausage, crumbled

2 cups thinly sliced shiitake and/or button mushrooms

¾ cup diced red bell peppers

½ teaspoon cracked black pepper

¼ teaspoon coarse salt

1 tablespoon garlic paste or finely minced garlic

1 teaspoon Italian seasoning or dry Italian salad dressing mix

1 cup grated Gruyère cheese

¾ cup ricotta cheese

¾ cup grated Parmesan cheese

½ cup sliced scallions

1 8-ounce package dried manicotti tubular shells

4 cups Real Deal Italian Meatless Sauce (page 30)

1 (8-ounce) package shredded mozzarella cheese

Place chicken and pork sausage in a large skillet over medium heat. Sauté for 2 minutes, until browned. Add mushrooms, diced peppers, black pepper, salt, garlic, and Italian seasoning. Cook for 5 minutes, stirring frequently, until vegetables are soft and moisture released from mushrooms has evaporated. Transfer mixture to a large bowl and allow it to cool for 5 minutes.

Mix Gruyère, ricotta, and Parmesan cheeses and scallions together in a medium bowl. Fold cheese mixture into chicken mixture. Place 1 cup tomato sauce in the bottom of a 4-quart slow cooker. Using a small spoon, stuff each dried manicotti tube with chicken-cheese mixture. Place half the stuffed manicotti tubes in a single layer in slow cooker. Spread 1 cup tomato sauce over first layer. Add second layer of stuffed tubes. Spread remaining 2 cups sauce over manicotti.

Cover slow cooker and cook on low setting for 4 to 5 hours, until manicotti are soft and sauce has thickened. Reduce heat setting to warm. Sprinkle mozzarella over manicotti, replace cover, and allow cheese to melt (about 15 minutes) before serving.

You can use bottled pasta sauce in this recipe, but to be authentically Italian, long-cooked homemade tomato "gravy" or "ragu" is de rigueur.

Serves: 6 to 8

Mexicana Lasagna   🕐 4–8

Far from a culture clash, this lasagna combines Mexican spiciness with the cheesy comfort of Italian cheeses. The no-cook lasagna noodles hold up better in a slow cooker than do Mexican tortillas. Top each serving with sour cream, if desired. It will calm the heat of the spicy chilies.

1 tablespoon olive oil
1 pound ground beef
1 cup chopped sweet onions, like Vidalia
1 teaspoon minced garlic
2 tablespoons Gourmet Garden Mexican Herb & Spice Blend paste
½ teaspoon salt
2 (10-ounce) cans Ro-Tel Diced Tomatoes & Green Chilies, with juices
1 (16-ounce) jar medium tomatillo salsa
1 (15-ounce) container part-skim ricotta cheese
2 (8-ounce) packages shredded mozzarella cheese
1 egg, beaten
1 (9-ounce) package flat no-cook lasagna noodles
½ cup grated Parmesan cheese
Sour cream

Heat oil in a large nonstick skillet over medium heat. Add ground beef, onions, and garlic. Cook, stirring frequently, until beef has browned completely, about 5 minutes. Drain beef mixture in a colander. Return mixture to skillet. Stir in herb and spice blend, salt, diced tomatoes, and salsa. Reduce heat to low and cook, stirring occasionally, for 10 minutes. Transfer beef mixture to a large bowl.

Place ricotta and mozzarella cheeses in a medium bowl. Add egg and stir until well blended.

Spread 1 cup meat sauce in the bottom of a 4-quart slow cooker. Break 3 dried lasagna noodles into pieces and place in an overlapping layer atop meat sauce. Spread 1 cup meat sauce over noodles. Using 2 teaspoons, place one-third cheese mixture in dollops atop sauce. Spread into an even layer with the back of a teaspoon.

Repeat layering: 3 noodles, broken in pieces; 1 cup meat sauce; one-third cheese mixture; 3 noodles, broken in pieces; 1 cup meat sauce; final one-third cheese mixture. Top cheese mixture with a layer of 3 more noodles, broken in pieces. Spread remaining meat sauce over noodles. Sprinkle Parmesan cheese over meat sauce. Cover slow cooker and cook on low setting for 5 hours, or until noodles are cooked through and lasagna layers hold together when tested with a sharp knife. (You can hold lasagna on warm setting for up to 30 minutes.)

To serve: Cut lasagna into wedges and serve immediately with sour cream on the side.

Layer lasagna in this easy order: meat sauce, noodles, meat sauce, cheese mixture, noodles, meat sauce, cheese mixture, noodles, meat sauce, cheese mixture, noodles, meat sauce.

Serves: 6 to 8

Moussaka

The origin of the word, "moussaka," is believed to be Arabic. Turkey, Lebanon, and other Middle Eastern countries have many versions of the dish, but all nations consider this sumptuous layering of eggplant, meat sauce, cheese, and white sauce a Greek classic.

2 pounds (about 3) graffiti eggplants (see opposite)

Olive oil spray

1 pound ground beef

1 cup chopped sweet onions, like Vidalia

1 teaspoon garlic paste or finely minced garlic

1 (8-ounce) can tomato sauce

1 (1.37-ounce) envelope McCormick Thick & Zesty Tomato Sauce Mix

¾ cup red wine

⅓ cup fresh bread crumbs

1 (8-ounce) package shredded Monterey Jack cheese (about 2 cups), divided

1 tablespoon butter

1 tablespoon flour

1 cup evaporated milk

Preheat oven to 250°F. Cut off top and bottom of each eggplant, then peel eggplants. Cut eggplants into ¼-inch-wide slices. Place eggplant slices on baking sheets and coat them liberally with olive oil spray. Bake for 10 minutes. Turn slices over and coat them liberally with olive oil spray. Bake for 10 minutes more. Remove eggplant slices from oven and divide them equally among 3 small plates. Set aside.

Place ground beef in a large nonstick skillet over medium heat. Sauté meat until browned, stirring occasionally, about 3 to 4 minutes. Drain browned beef in a colander and return it to skillet. Add onions and garlic and sauté for 1 minute, stirring constantly.

Stir in tomato sauce, tomato sauce mix, and wine. Reduce heat to low and simmer for 5 minutes, stirring occasionally. Remove from heat and set aside.

Sprinkle bread crumbs in the bottom of a 4-quart slow cooker. Place one-third of the eggplant slices in a layer atop crumbs. Spread one-half the meat mixture over eggplant. Sprinkle ½ cup shredded cheese over meat mixture. Repeat the layers: one-third eggplant slices, one-half meat mixture, ½ cup shredded cheese. Place final one-third eggplant slices in a layer atop cheese.

Melt butter in a small nonstick saucepan over medium-low heat. Whisk in flour to form a roux. Whisk in evaporated milk and keep whisking until it just comes to a boil, about 1 minute. Remove saucepan from heat and whisk in remaining cheese (about 1 cup). Pour cheese sauce over eggplant in slow cooker.

Cover slow cooker and cook on low setting for 3 to 3½ hours, until filling is firm and cheese sauce is crusty on top.

Graffiti eggplants are ivory with purple markings or purple with ivory markings. They are smooth and creamy when cooked and aren't as bitter as large purple-black eggplants tend to be. If you can't find them in your supermarket, substitute small, smooth-skinned purple-black eggplants, which will taste milder than their larger cousins.

Serves: 4 to 6

Mac 'n' Cheese with Caramelized Onions and Tomatoes

-4

Almost lasagna, this slow-cooked macaroni and cheese redefines the original concept from the '50s, elevating good old Velveeta cheese to a dish that pleases the adult palate.

½ tablespoon margarine

1 pound elbow macaroni or
    penne rigate pasta

1 (28-ounce) can crushed tomatoes
    with herbs

2 tablespoons butter

2 large sweet onions, like Vidalia, cut in half
    and thinly sliced (about 6 cups)

1 teaspoon sugar

2 (12-ounce) cans evaporated milk

1 teaspoon salt

½ teaspoon pepper

1 pound Velveeta cheese,
    cut into 1-inch chunks

2 eggs, beaten

Parmesan cheese

Liberally grease bottom and sides of a 6-quart slow cooker with margarine. Place uncooked macaroni and tomatoes into slow cooker. Stir to combine.

Melt butter in a large nonstick skillet over medium heat. Add onions. Sprinkle onions with sugar, and sauté, stirring occasionally, for 5 minutes. Reduce heat to medium-low and continue sautéing onions until they are soft and caramelized, about 15 minutes more. Transfer onions to slow cooker. Stir to combine with macaroni and tomatoes.

Place evaporated milk, salt, pepper, and cheese in large saucepan over medium-low heat. Cook, stirring frequently, until cheese has melted. Do not allow cheese sauce to boil. Remove from heat and pour cheese sauce into slow cooker. Stir to combine ingredients. Allow mixture to cool for 5 minutes. Stir in beaten eggs.

Cook on low setting for 3½ to 4 hours, until pasta has cooked through but is not mushy, and cheese sauce has thickened.

To serve: Cut mac 'n' cheese into wedges and serve each portion sprinkled with Parmesan cheese.

Only evaporated milk and processed cheese can withstand the long, slow-cooking process without curdling. The beaten eggs act as a thickening agent. You must allow cheese sauce mixture to cool for a few minutes so that the eggs won't cook when stirred into the macaroni and cheese sauce.

Serves: 8 to 10

Sides

- Braised Fennel Ragout – *Italy*
- Peperonata – *Italy*
- Tomato Bread Pudding – *USA*
- Hawaiian Candied Tomatoes – *USA*
- Sweet and Sour Baby Onions – *Italy*
- Garlic-Chive Mashed Potatoes – *USA*
- Cheesy Shredded Potatoes – *France*
- Stovie Potatoes – *Scotland*
- Mashed South African Sweet "Potats" – *South Africa*
- Persian Rice – *Middle East*
- Boston Baked Beans – *USA*
- Cuban Black Beans – *Cuba*
- Black-eyed Peas with Tomatoes, Mushrooms, and Onions – *India*

Braised Fennel Ragout

-4

One of the oft-forgotten vegetables in the United States, fennel is used extensively in European cuisines, especially that of France and Italy. Packed with nutrients and offering a subtle licorice or anise flavor, braised fennel makes a savory cushion on which to place grilled scallops.

1 large fennel bulb

1 tablespoon olive oil

2 teaspoons garlic paste or finely minced garlic

1 cup thinly sliced sweet onions, like Vidalia

5 large plum tomatoes, thinly sliced lengthwise, then cut in half lengthwise

2 tablespoons white wine

1 tablespoon honey

1 tablespoon orange juice concentrate

1 teaspoon salt

½ teaspoon black pepper

Cut stalks off fennel bulb and discard, or refrigerate for another use. Cut fennel bulb into ½-inch slices, crosswise. Remove small green center root from each slice and discard. Discard root end of bulb. Place fennel slices in a colander. Rinse with cold water and dry with paper toweling.

Place oil in a large nonstick skillet over medium heat. When oil is hot, add sliced fennel, garlic, and onions. Sauté for 3 minutes, stirring frequently. Add tomatoes, wine, honey, orange juice concentrate, salt, and pepper. Sauté for 2 minutes, stirring frequently.

Transfer fennel mixture to a 1½-quart slow cooker. Cook on low setting for 3 to 3½ hours, until fennel is tender.

The fennel stalks can be used in stocks, soups, and stews. Use the feathery leaves as an herbal seasoning, much as you would dill leaves.

Serves: 4 to 6

Peperonata

-4

This classic Sicilian dish is traditionally served as a room temperature side dish accompaniment for fish, chicken, beef, or grilled spicy Italian sausage. It is also served as a cold antipasto with sliced rustic bread. You can kick the spice up a notch by adding crushed red pepper flakes during the cooking process.

3 tablespoons olive oil, divided

2 red onions, halved and thinly sliced

1 tablespoon garlic paste or finely minced garlic

1 tablespoon Gourmet Garden Mediterranean Herb & Spice Blend paste

2 large red bell peppers, cored, seeded, and cut into thin strips

2 large yellow bell peppers, cored, seeded, and cut into thin strips

2 large orange bell peppers, cored, seeded, and cut into thin strips

10 large plum tomatoes, seeded and chopped

¼ cup capers, rinsed and drained

1 tablespoon plus 1 teaspoon red wine vinegar

Salt and black pepper

1 teaspoon Fox Point Seasoning (optional)

¾ cup snipped fresh basil

Place 2 tablespoons oil in a large nonstick skillet over medium heat. Add onions and sauté for 7 minutes, stirring frequently. Add garlic and herb pastes and sauté for 1 minute, stirring constantly. Transfer onion mixture to a 5-quart slow cooker. Place remaining 1 tablespoon oil in skillet. Add peppers and sauté for 3 minutes, stirring frequently, until peppers have softened. Transfer to slow cooker.

Add tomatoes, capers, vinegar, 2 teaspoons salt, 1 teaspoon black pepper, and Fox Point Seasoning to slow cooker. Stir to combine ingredients. Cover slow cooker and cook on low setting for 3 hours, until peppers have cooked through but are not mushy. Stir in basil and add salt and pepper to taste. Serve immediately or transfer to a covered container and refrigerate until needed. (Reheat gently in a large nonstick saucepan over low heat before serving.)

Fox Point Seasoning is a mixture of salt, shallots, chives, garlic, onions, and green peppercorns. It is available from Penzeys Spices: www.penzeys.com.

Serves: 8 to 10

Tomato Bread Pudding

 4–8

During the Civil War, bread pudding was popular on both sides of the Mason-Dixon Line, where the soldiers used scraps of bread and whatever ingredients they could find to rustle up a meal. Super sweet yet complex in flavor, this dish makes a great accompaniment to grilled meat, chicken, or seafood.

4 cups cubed stale sourdough bread (crusts removed)

½ cup melted butter

1 cup crushed tomato puree

1 cup dark brown sugar

¼ cup water

Place bread cubes in a 1½-quart slow cooker. Pour melted butter over bread. Place tomato puree, brown sugar, and water in a small nonstick saucepan over medium-low heat. Cook for 5 minutes, stirring frequently, until sugar dissolves. Pour tomato mixture over bread cubes and stir to combine.

Cover slow cooker and cook on low setting for 5 hours, until pudding is soufflé-like in texture. (You can hold pudding on warm setting for up to 1 hour.)

The bread cube mixture should be within an inch of the top of the slow cooker because it will cook down considerably. If you double or triple this recipe to serve more people, be sure to use a slow cooker that allows bread to initially almost fill the cooker insert. Otherwise, reduce cooking time because the dish will cook faster if the cooker is only partially full.

Serves: 4

Hawaiian Candied Tomatoes

 -4

Tomato lovers rejoice! These decadently sweet tomatoes — a favorite in the islands of our fiftieth state — taste almost like dessert. Serve them as a side dish with grilled steak or roast beef.

4 small ripe tomatoes

Salt

2 tablespoons butter

½ cup chopped sweet onions, like Vidalia

¼ cup light brown sugar

2 teaspoons honey

¼ teaspoon black pepper

1 cup fresh bread crumbs

2 teaspoons Parmesan cheese

Cut the top quarter off the stem end of each tomato. Scoop out seeds and liquid from seed cavities with a small spoon, taking care not to break the flesh between each cavity. Sprinkle inside of each tomato with salt and turn upside-down on paper toweling to drain.

Melt butter in a small nonstick skillet over medium heat. Add onions and sauté until softened, about 2 minutes. Stir in brown sugar, honey, ¼ teaspoon salt, and pepper. Add bread crumbs and stir until well coated with butter sauce. Using a small spoon, stuff each tomato with one-quarter of the mixture, tucking it into the seed cavities and mounding stuffing in the tomato.

Coat a 1½-quart slow cooker with vegetable cooking spray. Place tomatoes in slow cooker, cover, and cook on low setting for 2 to 2½ hours, until tomatoes have softened but are not mushy. Hold on warm setting for up to 30 minutes or serve immediately.

To serve: Sprinkle the top of each stuffed tomato with ½ teaspoon Parmesan cheese.

Make fresh bread crumbs in your food processor, using leftover bits of bread. Store crumbs in a zipper bag in the freezer until needed.

Serves: 4

Sweet and Sour Baby Onions

🕐 4–8

Balsamic vinegar dates back to Modena, Italy, in the 11th century, when barrels of the prized, dark vinegar were often included in a lady's dowry. Really good balsamic vinegar — especially that known as aceto balsamico *— is very expensive. In this recipe, I've substituted white balsamic vinegar from Modena. It is not aged in wooden barrels (which makes it less expensive) and its dark color is filtered out (which makes it crystal clear). But its distinctive sweet-sour flavor is the perfect foil for these tiny onions.*

2 (1-pound) bags frozen peeled white pearl onions

1 extra-large chicken bouillon cube (about ½ ounce)

2 tablespoons butter, melted

2 tablespoons white balsamic vinegar

1 tablespoon sugar

Salt and freshly ground black pepper

1½ teaspoons cornstarch

Place frozen onions in a 4-quart slow cooker. Crumble bouillon cube into a small bowl. Whisk in butter, vinegar, and sugar. Pour mixture over onions and stir to combine. Cover slow cooker and cook on low setting for 4 to 4½ hours. Add salt and pepper to taste, stir onions, re-cover, and cook for 30 more minutes.

Strain onions in a sieve placed over a small glass bowl. Place onions in a serving bowl. Whisk cornstarch into onion liquid. Microwave liquid until it thickens, about 1 to 2 minutes. Pour sauce over onions and toss to combine.

🕐 These little onions are great served as a side dish with roast pork or turkey. Use leftovers on a skewer with olives and smoked sausage bites for a quick appetizer.

Serves: 6

Garlic-Chive Mashed Potatoes

 4–8

These potatoes are so tasty, creamy, and easy to prepare, I'll never make them on the stovetop again. For different flavored potatoes, try replacing the chives with other snipped fresh herbs, like dill, parsley, thyme, or basil.

3 pounds Yukon Gold potatoes, peeled and cut into 2-inch chunks

1 cup chopped onions, like Vidalia

5 teaspoons garlic paste or finely minced garlic

2 tablespoons olive oil

1 teaspoon salt

⅛ teaspoon black pepper

⅔ cup water

2 tablespoons butter, cut into small pieces

1 (8-ounce) package cream cheese, softened to room temperature

2 tablespoons snipped fresh chives or 2 teaspoons dried

Place potatoes in a 4-quart slow cooker. Sprinkle onions over potatoes. Whisk garlic, olive oil, salt, and pepper together in a small bowl. Pour over potatoes. Pour water over potatoes. Stir to mix ingredients well. Cover and cook on high setting for 4 hours, until potatoes are fork-tender.

Mash potatoes with a masher or a fork. Sprinkle butter over mashed potatoes. When butter has melted, add cream cheese. Stir until smooth and creamy. Sprinkle potatoes with chives and stir to mix well.

Transfer potatoes to a serving bowl and serve immediately or cover slow cooker and hold potatoes on warm setting for up to 2 hours.

For more rustic-looking mashed potatoes, use small red potatoes. Cut them in half and leave the skins on.

Serves: 6 to 8

Cheesy Shredded Potatoes

🕐 4–8

Reminiscent of the flavor of a French potato gratin, these potatoes are as comforting as they are easy to prepare.

1 (30-ounce) package frozen country-style hash brown shredded potatoes, thawed
½ cup (8 tablespoons) melted butter, divided
1 (8-ounce) package shredded sharp cheddar cheese
1 (10.75-ounce) can Campbell's Cream of Chicken Soup with Herbs
1½ tablespoons dried minced onions
¾ cup sour cream
1 cup fresh bread crumbs

Squeeze thawed potatoes with paper toweling to remove excess moisture. Place potatoes in a 4-quart slow cooker. Add ¼ cup (4 tablespoons) melted butter, cheese, soup, and dried minced onions. Stir until ingredients are well combined. Cover slow cooker and cook on low temperature for 3½ hours. Stir in sour cream. Top with bread crumbs and drizzle remaining ¼ cup melted butter over crumbs. Re-cover slow cooker, and cook potatoes for 30 minutes more, until crumbs have browned slightly.

🕐 You can reduce heat setting to warm and hold potatoes for up to 2 hours.
Serves: 6 to 8

Stovie Potatoes

 4–8

Stovies are a traditional Scottish dish, slowly cooked in a covered cast-iron skillet. Good stovies must be cooked for several hours without letting them burn on the bottom and stick to the skillet. Tradition mandates that the lid must never be lifted during the cooking time. Perfectly suited for conversion to a slow cooker, these thinly sliced seasoned potatoes cook for several hours bathed in melted butter.

½ cup grated Parmesan cheese

¼ cup flour

¼ teaspoon seasoning blend, like McCormick Vegetable Supreme or Lemon-Herb

¼ teaspoon black pepper

6 tablespoons plus 1 teaspoon butter, divided

3 large Yukon Gold potatoes

Salt

Mix cheese, flour, seasoning blend, and pepper together in a medium bowl. Grease bottom and sides of a 2-quart slow cooker with 1 teaspoon butter.

Working with 1 potato at a time, peel potato and cut into ¼-inch slices. Dredge potato slices in cheese-flour mixture, making sure both sides are well coated. Place slices in an overlapping layer in the bottom of the slow cooker. Sprinkle with salt to taste. Divide butter into 3 equal parts (about 2 tablespoons each). Cut 1 portion of butter into 18 small pieces (3 slices, each cut into 6 pieces). Sprinkle butter over potatoes.

Repeat with two more layers of coated potatoes, salt, and butter. Sprinkle any remaining cheese-flour mixture over potatoes.

Cover slow cooker and cook on low setting for 6 to 8 hours, until potatoes are cooked through and bubbly, but not mushy.

Some authentic stovie potatoes are layered with onions as well. If you'd like to add onions, thinly slice a large sweet onion, like Vidalia. Sauté onions in 1 tablespoon butter in a large nonstick skillet for about 3 minutes, until onions are soft. Divide onions equally and place them atop each potato layer. To serve 6 to 8, double recipe, making 6 layers instead of 3 layers, and cook in a 4-quart slow cooker.

Serves: 4

Mashed South African Sweet "Potats"

 4–8

South Africans enjoy eating something sweet with their meat course and sweet "potats" fill the bill. A delicate combination of brown sugar, orange, gingerroot, sherry, and cinnamon seasons the sweet potatoes. In South Africa, the potatoes would actually be yams, which are rarely grown in the U.S.

4 cups peeled, cubed sweet potatoes (2 to 3 potatoes)

¼ cup orange juice

1 stick cinnamon

1 teaspoon dried grated orange peel

6 tablespoons melted butter

½ cup light brown sugar

2 thin slices peeled gingerroot, cut into slivers

1 tablespoon cream sherry

2 tablespoons finely chopped pecans (optional)

Mix sweet potatoes, orange juice, cinnamon stick, orange peel, butter, brown sugar, gingerroot, and sherry in a 1½-quart slow cooker. Cook on low setting for 4 to 4½ hours, until potatoes are fork-tender.

Remove cinnamon stick and discard. Transfer sweet potatoes and cooking liquid to a food processor. Pulse until potatoes are smooth.

To serve: Transfer potatoes to a serving dish. Sprinkle with pecans if desired.

You can substitute 2 pinches of dried ground ginger for the fresh in this recipe. If you'd like to use grated fresh orange peel, increase amount to 1 tablespoon.

Serves: 4 to 6

Persian Rice

-4

Unlike conventional rice preparations, Persian rice is first boiled, then rinsed and drained, and finally slowly steamed until each individual grain is fluffy and the bottom layer of rice is golden brown. Traditionally the rice is inverted onto a platter, like an upside-down cake. In a Persian household, the crunchy tadik *that tops the rice "cake" is the most coveted part of the meal.*

3 cups basmati rice

2 teaspoons salt

2 tablespoons butter

10 threads saffron, ground with mortar and pestle

Place rice in a nonstick, stovetop-safe, 5-quart slow cooker insert. Cover rice with water and, with your hands, agitate the rice, releasing the starch. Pour off the cloudy water and repeat this process until the water is clear. Pour off the water a final time, then add cold water to 3 inches above the rice (about 12 cups).

Cover slow cooker insert and place on stovetop burner over high heat. Bring rice and water to a rolling boil (keep an eye on this, as it can boil over quickly). Reduce heat to medium, remove cover, and boil rice, stirring occasionally, until it softens, starts to puff, and is al dente to the taste, about 5 to 7 minutes. Meanwhile, dissolve saffron in 2 tablespoons hot water.

Remove insert from burner and drain rice in a colander. Rinse drained rice with cold water and drain again. Wipe out the insert with paper toweling to remove any starch residue. Return it to the burner over medium heat. Add butter. When butter is melted, stir in saffron water. Add drained rice to the pot. With the handle of the spoon, poke 5 holes in the rice to the bottom of the pan. When steam rises from the holes, transfer insert to slow cooker. Place 3 pieces of paper toweling atop slow cooker insert, making sure all edges are covered. Cover and press down on the lid so the slow cooker is sealed completely. Cook on low setting for 2 hours. (You can hold rice on warm setting for up to 2 hours.)

To serve: Remove insert from slow cooker. Remove lid and paper toweling. Place a large oval platter over insert. Gripping both handles and platter, upend contents of insert onto platter. Rice will be held together in a large cake by the crispy covering of *tadik*.

If you don't have a stovetop-safe slow cooker, boil the rice in a large nonstick saucepan. Place melted butter and saffron water in a conventional 5½-quart slow cooker, add rice, and proceed with directions as written. The rice freezes very well. Divide leftover rice into meal-size portions and freeze in airtight containers. Simply microwave to reheat.

Serves: 12 to 16

Boston Baked Beans

 4–8

These famous beans have a lesser-known cousin . . . Vermont baked beans. The difference lies in one crucial ingredient. Vermonters insist that maple syrup be used instead of molasses. To make a New England compromise, substitute 2½ tablespoons molasses and 2½ tablespoons maple syrup for the amount of molasses called for in this recipe.

1 (16-ounce) can Bush's Chili Beans (pinto beans in chili sauce)
2 (15.5-ounce) cans Great Northern beans, drained, rinsed, and drained again
2 (16-ounce) cans Bush's Mixed Beans, drained, rinsed, and drained again
8 slices center-cut bacon, cut in ½-inch dice
5 teaspoons garlic paste or finely minced garlic
1 cup chopped sweet onions, like Vidalia
1 tablespoon Worcestershire sauce
2 tablespoons cider vinegar
¾ cup ketchup
¼ cup plus 2 tablespoons dark brown sugar
1 teaspoon dry mustard
5 tablespoons molasses

Place beans in a 4-quart slow cooker. Fry bacon in a large nonstick skillet over medium heat until crispy. Remove bacon with a slotted spoon and let it drain on paper toweling. Transfer bacon to slow cooker.

Add garlic and onions to skillet and sauté over medium heat, stirring frequently, for about 1½ minutes, until onions are soft but not brown. (If you don't have enough bacon grease to cook garlic and onions, add 1 tablespoon olive oil.) Reduce heat to medium-low. Add Worcestershire sauce, vinegar, ketchup, brown sugar, dry mustard, and molasses. Stir to mix well. Cook sauce, stirring constantly, until it just reaches a boil, about 1½ minutes. Transfer sauce to slow cooker.

Stir until ingredients are well mixed. Cover slow cooker and cook for 5½ to 6 hours on low setting.

Center-cut bacon is leaner than regular bacon, thereby releasing less grease. If you use regular bacon, use only 6 pieces and discard all but 1 tablespoon bacon grease before sautéing the garlic and onions.

Serves: 4 to 6

Cuban Black Beans

4–8

Frijoles negros, or black beans, are a staple in Cuba as well as other islands of the Caribbean. Cubans often serve the beans topped with a cupful of hot yellow rice. Dried black beans must be picked through carefully to remove discolored or misshapen ones and then must be rinsed thoroughly. Soak the beans for at least 10 hours to rehydrate them before they are cooked.

1 (14-ounce) package dried black beans	1 teaspoon dried marjoram
1½ teaspoons salt, divided	¼ teaspoon black pepper
2 tablespoons olive oil	1 teaspoon sugar
2 cups chopped sweet onions, like Vidalia	½ teaspoon cider vinegar
2 cups chopped green bell peppers	1 packet Goya or Badia sazón (coriander
4 teaspoons garlic paste	and annatto seasoning, see below)
or finely minced garlic	2 bay leaves

One day ahead: Sort through beans, discarding broken ones. Rinse and drain beans. Place beans in a large bowl. Add water to cover beans by 3 inches. Cover bowl with plastic wrap and allow beans to soak at room temperature overnight.

To cook: Place beans and soaking water in a 5-quart slow cooker. Add 1 teaspoon salt. Cover slow cooker and cook on high setting for 3 hours, until beans are tender. (Test tenderness by pinching a bean between your thumb and index finger. If the bean feels soft and it splits when pinched, it is done.) Drain beans in a colander, reserving 1 cup cooking liquid. Return beans to slow cooker.

Place olive oil in a large nonstick skillet over medium heat. When oil is hot, add onions, green peppers, garlic, marjoram, ½ teaspoon salt, pepper, sugar, vinegar, and sazón. Sauté, stirring frequently, for 4 to 5 minutes or until onions and peppers soften and mixture is fragrant. Transfer vegetable mixture to slow cooker. Add bay leaves and reserved cooking liquid. Stir until ingredients are well mixed.

Re-cover slow cooker and cook on low setting for 3 more hours. Remove bay leaves before serving. Adjust seasoning by adding salt and pepper to taste.

Both Goya and Badia brands make a sazón (seasoning) blend of coriander, annatto, salt, garlic, dehydrated onion, paprika, and other Spanish spices. It usually can be found in the Spanish section of your supermarket or at a Spanish grocery. Or find it at: www.badia-spices.com or www.goya.com.

Serves: 8 to 10 (makes 6 cups)

Black-eyed Peas with Tomatoes, Mushrooms, and Onions

 8+

If you thought black-eyed peas were only served in the American South, think again. A popular side dish served in India, these black-eyed peas are delicately yet pungently seasoned with cumin, coriander, and turmeric — ubiquitous herbs and spices of the region. Serve it as a vegetarian dish or with the Indian beef stew called Rogan Josh (page 44).

1¾ cups dried black-eyed peas

1 (32-ounce) carton mushroom broth

1 cup water

3 tablespoons canola oil

1 (1-inch) stick cinnamon

1 teaspoon cumin seeds

4 teaspoons garlic paste or finely minced garlic

2 cups chopped sweet onions, like Vidalia

2 cups sliced button mushrooms

2 cups quartered cherry tomatoes

2 teaspoons dried coriander leaves

½ teaspoon ground cumin

½ teaspoon ground turmeric

¼ teaspoon cayenne pepper

2 teaspoons salt

3 tablespoons snipped fresh parsley or cilantro

The day before: Pick over dried peas, discarding any broken ones. Place peas in a medium bowl and add water to cover peas by 3 inches. Set aside at room temperature to soak overnight.

Early in the morning: Drain peas in a colander, rinse with cold water, and drain again. Transfer peas to a 4-quart slow cooker. Add mushroom broth and 1 cup water. Cover slow cooker and cook on low setting for 8 to 10 hours, until peas are al dente to the bite. Drain peas in a colander, then return them to slow cooker.

Place oil, cinnamon stick, and cumin seeds in a large nonstick skillet over medium heat. When oil starts to sizzle, add garlic and onions. Sauté, stirring occasionally, until onions have softened, about 3 minutes. Add mushrooms and sauté for 3 minutes more, stirring occasionally. Add tomatoes, coriander, ground cumin, turmeric, cayenne, and salt. Stir to combine. Reduce heat to low and cook for 8 minutes, stirring occasionally. Transfer tomato mixture to slow cooker. Stir until all ingredients are well combined.

Cook on low setting for 2 to 2½ hours, until black-eyed peas are tender. Remove cinnamon stick, sprinkle with fresh parsley or cilantro, and serve immediately.

Be sure to use dried coriander leaves, not ground coriander. Pacific Natural Foods brand makes a good mushroom broth. If you can't find mushroom broth, substitute vegetable broth. If you can't find cumin seeds, substitute ½ teaspoon ground cumin.

Serves: 4 to 6

Snacks and Desserts

Snacks

- Black Bean Dip – *Cuba*
- Buffalo Chicken Dip – *USA*
- Nacho Dip – *Texas/Mexico*
- Chutney-Sauced Cocktail Meatballs – *India*
- Brown Sugar Beer Sausage – *Germany*

Desserts

- Strawberry-Blueberry Crumble – *USA*
- Peach Crumble – *USA*
- Sugar Apple Crisp – *USA*
- Baked Apples – *Northern Hemisphere*
- Brandied Vanilla-Bean Applesauce – *USA*
- Orange-Rhubarb Bread "Pud" – *England*
- Rummy Apricot-Currant Bread Pudding – *France*

Black Bean Dip

-4

This slightly spicy black bean concoction is great dipped right out of the slow cooker with Tostito's Scoops. Or make baked nachos. Place white tortilla chips on a large nonstick baking sheet in a single layer. Spread black bean dip over tortilla chips. Top with your choice of sliced olives, chopped onions, diced fresh tomatoes, or minced jalapeños. Sprinkle with more shredded cheese and bake for 5 minutes in a 400°F oven.

1 (15-ounce) can black beans, rinsed and drained

1 jalapeño pepper, finely chopped

¼ cup chopped sweet onion, like Vidalia

½ cup thick and chunky medium-spicy jarred salsa

¼ cup sour cream

1¼ cups finely shredded Four Cheese Mexican Blend (2% milk)

Tostitos Scoops chips

Place beans, chopped jalapeño, onions, and salsa in a 1 to 1 ½-quart slow cooker. Cook on low setting for 2 to 3 hours. Reduce heat setting to warm. Stir in sour cream and shredded cheese. Serve immediately or hold on warm setting for 30 minutes.

To serve: Serve hot dip from slow cooker with Tostitos Scoops. Replace cover between servings.

Cheese and sour cream tend to curdle if cooked in the slow cooker for a long time. Adding them at the end of the cooking cycle and reducing heat to warm keeps the mixture creamy. You can substitute 2 cups Cuban Black Beans (page 123) for the canned black beans.

Serves: 6 to 8

Buffalo Chicken Dip

-4

Legend has it that Buffalo chicken wings were first made as a late-night throw-together snack at the Anchor Bar in Buffalo, New York, by co-owner Teressa Belissimo. This easy knockoff offers the same spicy kick as the original, but is bathed in creamy cheese dip.

2 (8-ounce) packages cream cheese

1 cup (8 fluid ounces) Frank's Red Hot Buffalo Sauce or other spicy chicken wing sauce

3 cups finely diced rotisserie chicken

1½ cups (12 fluid ounces) prepared ranch dressing

2 cups shredded sharp cheddar cheese

2 cups shredded mozzarella cheese

Tostitos Scoops or celery sticks

Place cream cheese and buffalo sauce in a medium saucepan over medium heat. Cook, stirring constantly, until cream cheese has melted. Transfer to a large bowl. Stir in chicken and ranch dressing. Transfer to a 1½- or 2-quart slow cooker. Cook on low setting for 1 to 1½ hours, until dip has heated through. Stir in shredded cheeses.

To serve: Reduce heat setting to warm and serve hot dip with Tostitos Scoops or celery sticks. Make sure cover is replaced between servings.

The shredded cheese has a tendency to curdle if cooked for a long period of time in a slow cooker. The cheese will melt quickly when stirred into the hot chicken mixture.

Serves: A crowd

Nacho Dip

-4

Tex-Mex at its best! Quick, easy, warm, and satisfying — everybody loves nachos!

1 cup leftover chili (pages 21–23) or Sloppy Joes (page 57)

1 (8-ounce) package cream cheese, softened

1 cup peeled, seeded, chopped fresh tomato

¼ cup seeded, minced jalapeño peppers

½ cup minced red onions

1 cup shredded sharp cheddar cheese

Tostitos Scoops chips

Place cold chili or Sloppy Joes in a 1½-quart slow cooker. Spread cream cheese on top. Top with tomatoes, then jalapeños, onions, and cheese. Cook for 2 hours on low setting. Reduce heat to warm setting and stir to mix ingredients.

To serve: Serve hot dip from slow cooker with Tostitos Scoops chips.

If you don't have any leftover chili or Sloppy Joes in your freezer, substitute 1 cup refried beans.

Serves: 12 to 16

Chutney-Sauced Cocktail Meatballs 4–8

Miniature meatballs are a hit at any cocktail party. This hearty hors d'oeuvre swims in a piquant Indian-inspired sauce. Homemade Peach Chutney (page 32) makes the sauce extra special, but you can substitute bottled chutney in a pinch.

1 cup Peach Chutney (page 32)

1 cup ketchup

1 (8-ounce) can tomato sauce

2 teaspoons gingerroot paste or finely minced gingerroot

½ cup dark brown sugar

1¼ pounds lean ground beef

½ cup panko bread crumbs

1 tablespoon dried minced onions

½ teaspoon salt

⅛ teaspoon pepper

¼ cup evaporated milk

1 egg, beaten

Mix together chutney, ketchup, tomato sauce, gingerroot, and brown sugar in a medium bowl. Transfer to a 2-quart slow cooker.

Place ground beef, bread crumbs, onions, salt, pepper, evaporated milk, and egg in a large bowl. Mix ingredients together well with clean hands. Roll beef mixture into 1-inch balls, the size of walnuts. Place meatballs in slow cooker, poking them into the sauce so that they are not overlapping each other but are covered with sauce.

Cover slow cooker and cook on low setting for 4 to 4½ hours, until meatballs are cooked through and sauce is rich and creamy. Serve immediately (in slow cooker) or refrigerate in a covered container until needed. (Place meatballs and sauce in a large saucepan and reheat gently on low heat; transfer to 2-quart slow cooker on warm setting to serve.) Guests should re-cover slow cooker between servings.

Meatballs should be served hot, in the sauce. Place fondue forks next to the slow cooker so that guests can spear the meatballs.

Serves: 8 to 10 as an hors d'oeuvre

Brown Sugar Beer Sausage

 4–8

This tasty hors d'oeuvre couldn't be easier to prepare. It is the perfect accompaniment to Gouda cheese.

2 cups brown sugar

1 (12-ounce) can beer (lager)

1 pound smoked sausage, cut into ½-inch-thick slices

1 tablespoon cornstarch

Early in the day or one day ahead: Place brown sugar and beer in a 1½-quart slow cooker. Whisk until sugar has dissolved. Add sausage slices. Stir to combine. Cover slow cooker and cook on low setting for 5 hours. Transfer sausages and liquid to a covered container and refrigerate for several hours or overnight, until grease congeals on the top.

To serve: Remove grease with a spoon and discard. Remove sausages with a slotted spoon and place in a medium bowl. Reserve liquid. Place cornstarch in a small bowl. Whisk in 2 tablespoons of liquid, forming a smooth paste. Place rest of reserved liquid in a medium nonstick saucepan over medium heat. Whisk in cornstarch mixture. Bring to a boil, stirring occasionally. Reduce heat to medium-low and cook for 10 minutes, stirring frequently. (Liquid will thicken and caramelize.) Add sausages and simmer until they are heated through, about 3 minutes. Transfer sausages and sauce to 1½-quart slow cooker and hold on warm for up to 3 hours. Place fondue forks next to slow cooker so guests can spear the sausages. Guests should re-cover slow cooker between servings.

You can make this appetizer several days ahead and refrigerate in a covered container until needed. Or cool sausages and sauce to room temperature, transfer to a covered container, and freeze for up to 1 month. Reheat thawed hors d'oeuvre gently in a small nonstick saucepan over low heat before transferring to slow cooker for serving.

Serves: 6 to 8

Strawberry-Blueberry Crumble

-4

Summertime, summertime . . . Serve this scrumptious berry crumble with a dollop of whipped cream or a scoop of vanilla ice cream. Although a little decadent, it is also fantastic for breakfast!

8 tablespoons butter, softened at room temperature

½ cup plus ⅔ cup light brown sugar, divided

¼ teaspoon ground cinnamon

½ teaspoon salt, divided

⅔ cup quick-cooking rolled oats

¾ cup flour, divided

4 cups sliced strawberries, washed and patted dry with paper toweling

2 dry pints blueberries, washed and patted dry with paper toweling

1 teaspoon grated lemon peel

1 teaspoon fresh lemon juice

Up to 8 hours ahead: Place butter, ½ cup brown sugar, cinnamon, and ¼ teaspoon salt in a medium bowl. Beat with an electric hand-held mixer or stir with a spoon until smooth. Add oats and ½ cup flour and beat or stir until well mixed. Cover topping mixture with plastic wrap and refrigerate until needed.

Place berries in a large bowl. Mix ⅔ cup brown sugar, ¼ cup flour, and ¼ teaspoon salt together in a medium bowl. Add to berries and toss gently with a large spoon until berries are well coated with the mixture. Stir grated lemon peel and lemon juice into berries.

Transfer berries to a 4-quart slow cooker. Remove topping mixture from refrigerator. Using clean hands, crumble topping evenly over fruit in slow cooker. Cover slow cooker insert with plastic wrap, if desired, and refrigerate until needed.

To cook: Remove insert from refrigerator 2½ hours before serving. Allow berry mixture to sit at room temperature for 30 minutes. Remove plastic wrap and place insert in slow cooker. Cover and cook on low setting for 2 hours. When berry mixture is bubbly, serve immediately or reduce heat setting to warm and hold for up to 1 hour.

🕐 Placing the topping in the refrigerator while you prepare the berry filling allows the butter in the topping to firm up a little, making it easier to crumble the topping over berries.

Serves: 8

Peach Crumble

 4–8

Desserts don't get any easier than this, a true fix-it-and-forget-it recipe. Serve it hot out of the slow cooker, topped with ice cream, frozen yogurt, or whipped cream.

½ tablespoon margarine
1 (21-ounce) can peach pie filling
1 (1-pound) bag frozen sliced peaches
1 tablespoon peach schnapps
1 (18.25-ounce) package Betty Crocker Super Moist Butter Yellow Cake Mix
¾ cup chopped pecans
½ cup butter, melted

Coat bottom and sides of a 4-quart slow cooker with margarine. Spread peach pie filling in bottom of slow cooker. Top with sliced peaches. Sprinkle schnapps over peaches.

Stir cake mix and pecans together in a large bowl. Add melted butter and stir mixture with a fork. Sprinkle cake mixture over fruit mixture. Cover slow cooker and cook on low setting for 4 to 4½ hours, until fruit is bubbly and cake mixture is crumbly and cooked through. Serve immediately or hold on warm setting for up to 1 hour.

You can get creative with this recipe. Pair different pie fillings with matching fresh or frozen fruit. Sprinkle fruit with corresponding liqueurs. Examples: cherry pie filling, frozen sour cherries, cherry liqueur; apple pie filling, sliced apples, amaretto liqueur.

Serves: 6

Sugar Apple Crisp

 -4

You don't need to wait for apple season to make this All-American dessert. Granny Smith apples are available all year long.

5 large Granny Smith apples, peeled, cored, and sliced (3 pounds)

¼ cup melted butter, divided

1 teaspoon grated lemon peel

1 tablespoon grated orange peel

2 tablespoons Grand Marnier or other orange liqueur

2 tablespoons Amaretto or other almond liqueur

1 (3.4-ounce) package Jell-O French Vanilla Instant Pudding Mix

1 teaspoon ground cinnamon

½ cup chopped Nilla Wafers

¼ cup sliced almonds

¼ cup sugar

Place apple slices in a large bowl. Pour 2 tablespoons melted butter over apples and toss to combine. Sprinkle grated lemon and orange peels and liqueurs over apples. Toss to combine.

Mix pudding mix and cinnamon together in a medium bowl. Add mixture to apples in thirds, tossing to combine ingredients between each addition.

Transfer apple mixture to a 4- or 5-quart slow cooker. Cover slow cooker and cook on low setting for 3½ hours, until apples are soft and mixture is bubbly. Reduce heat setting to warm and hold for up to 1 hour.

Meanwhile, place remaining 2 tablespoons melted butter in a small nonstick skillet over low heat. Add Nilla Wafer crumbs, almonds, and sugar. Cook mixture, stirring constantly, for 1½ minutes. Remove skillet from heat. Allow mixture to cool in the skillet. Stir occasionally.

To serve: Place a portion of the apple crisp in a shallow dessert bowl. Sprinkle the almond-crumb mixture over apples. Serve immediately.

An apple peeler/corer machine makes fast work of the apple prep in this recipe. You'll find one in kitchen supply stores for about $20.

Serves: 8

Baked Apples

🕐 4–8

In apple-producing countries of the Northern Hemisphere, nothing spells autumn like baked apples. Look for Pink Lady, Honeycrisp, or other sweet-tart varieties at your local farmers' market.

2 tablespoons melted butter, divided
4 medium sweet-tart apples, washed, peeled, and cored
½ cup white granulated sugar or demerara sugar
6 tablespoons apricot preserves
Ice cream

Brush inside of a 2-quart slow cooker with some of the melted butter. Working with 1 apple at a time, brush apple with remaining butter. Place sugar in a shallow bowl. Roll buttered apple in sugar. Place apple in slow cooker. Spoon 1½ tablespoons apricot preserves into cored cavity of apple. Repeat with remaining apples. Sprinkle remaining sugar over apples in slow cooker.

Cover slow cooker and cook on low setting for 5 hours, until apples are soft, cooked through, and lightly browned. (You can keep apples in slow cooker on warm setting for up to 2 hours.)

To serve: Place 1 apple on each of 4 dessert plates. Place a scoop of your favorite ice cream next to apple. Serve immediately.

🕐 Demerara sugar is a light brown sugar with large golden crystals. You can usually find it in the sugar section of your supermarket. Use an apple peeler/corer machine if you have one. The apples will end up sliced as well, but they will hold together if you peel only the top two-thirds of the apple.

Serves: 4

Brandied Vanilla-Bean Applesauce ⏱ 4–8

Macouns, a Northeast regional favorite developed in New York state in the 1920s, are found only during the months of October and November at farmers' markets, roadside stands, or specialty markets such as Trader Joe's, Whole Foods, or Fresh Market. (You can order them online at www.honeycrispapples.org.) The more readily available Jonagold or Honeycrisp are great substitutes.

2 cups apple juice
10 sweet-tart apples, like Macoun, Jonagold, or Honeycrisp
3 tablespoons butter, melted
4 tablespoons sugar
2 tablespoons brandy
½ vanilla bean, cut lengthwise

Place apple juice in a large bowl. Peel, core, and thinly slice apples. Place them immediately into the bowl of apple juice so that they don't turn brown. Drain apple slices in a colander, reserving 3 tablespoons apple juice.

Return apple slices to empty bowl. Add reserved apple juice, butter, sugar, and brandy. Toss to combine. Place mixture in a 4- to 5-quart slow cooker. Bury vanilla bean in the middle of the apple slices.

Cook on low setting for 4 hours, until apples can be broken up with a wooden spoon into a coarse sauce. Remove vanilla bean and discard. Serve warm or refrigerate in a covered container for up to 1 week or freeze for up to 2 months.

🕐 Although great-tasting on its own, this applesauce is super as an accompaniment for pork roast or chops, on top of French toast, or as a filling for crêpes or puff pastry shells.

Makes: 4 cups

Orange-Rhubarb Bread "Pud"

-4

Cultivated rhubarb has been used medicinally in China for more than 5,000 years. Botanically considered a vegetable — not a fruit — rhubarb was not widely used for culinary purposes until the early 19th century, when it became a popular dessert ingredient in England. The addition of oranges takes this English bread pudding ("pud") out of the ordinary.

1 navel orange

1½ to 2 cups (½-inch) diced rhubarb

1 tablespoon Minute Tapioca

¾ cup sugar

2 cups (½-inch) cubed white bread

3 tablespoons melted butter

¼ cup unsweetened coconut

Grate orange peel with a microplane. Set aside. Peel orange, slice, and cut orange into ½-inch dice, reserving juices. Set aside.

Place rhubarb, tapioca, sugar, bread cubes, melted butter, diced oranges with juices, 2 tablespoons grated orange peel, and coconut in a medium bowl. Stir until well mixed. Transfer to a 1½- or 2-quart slow cooker. (Wrap remaining grated orange peel in plastic wrap and freeze to use at another time.)

Cook on low setting for 3 hours. (You can hold pudding on warm setting for up to 1 hour.)

To serve: Serve warm, with a scoop of vanilla ice cream, a dollop of whipped cream, or a splash of heavy cream.

Two stalks of rhubarb equal about 1 cup diced. To serve a larger group, double the recipe and place in a 4-quart slow cooker. Cooking time remains the same. Some super-markets sell diced rhubarb in bags in the frozen food section. You do not need to defrost the rhubarb before using it in this recipe.

Serves: 4

Rummy Apricot-Currant Bread Pudding 4–8

The French are renowned for transforming stale bread and pantry items into stunning desserts. This bread pudding showcases rum-soaked dried fruits. The type of bread you use determines the texture of the resulting pudding: country-style, chewy bread will yield a soufflé-like pudding, while soft, dense bread will create a more compact dessert.

½ cup dried currants	1 teaspoon vanilla extract
1 cup chopped dried apricots	⅜ teaspoon salt
⅓ cup dark rum, like Myers's	1 cup sugar, divided
2 (12-ounce) cans evaporated milk (3 cups)	2 tablespoons butter, divided
3 large eggs	10 (½-inch-thick) slices stale bread

The day before: Place currants and apricots in a small bowl. Stir in rum, cover bowl with plastic wrap, and allow to sit overnight at room temperature so that dried fruits absorb the rum and plump up.

Early in the day: Place evaporated milk in a large bowl. Whisk in eggs, one at a time. Whisk in vanilla, salt, and all but 4½ tablespoons of the sugar. Set aside. Drain the currants and apricots, reserving liquid. Whisk drained liquid into milk mixture. Set aside 1 tablespoon of the fruit mixture in a small bowl.

Liberally grease a 4-quart slow cooker with butter, then cut remaining butter into small pieces and set aside. Place one-third of the bread slices in the bottom of the slow cooker, pressing so that bread covers the entire surface. Sprinkle with one-third of the currants and apricots. Pour one-third of the milk mixture over fruit and bread. Repeat layering two more times: bread, fruit, milk.

Mix reserved 4½ tablespoons sugar and 1 tablespoon fruit together. Sprinkle over pudding. Dot the top of pudding with the small pieces of butter.

Cover slow cooker and cook on low setting for 4 hours, or until a knife inserted in the center comes out clean.

To serve: Scoop bread pudding into bowls and serve warm.

You can substitute dried raisins, cherries, cranberries, figs, or your other favorite dried fruits in this recipe.

Serves: 6 to 8

STOCKING THE PANTRY, 'FRIDGE, AND FREEZER

Pantry

PRODUCE

bananas

garlic

potatoes: white, new, red

shallots

squash (butternut)

sweet potatoes: white, orange

tomatoes: slicing, grape, cherry, plum or Roma

BAKING SUPPLIES

cake mix (Betty Crocker Super Moist Butter Yellow)

cornstarch

extracts (vanilla)

flour (all-purpose)

Jell-O Pudding (French Vanilla)

Minute Tapioca

pie fillings: pumpkin, no-sugar-added cherry, peach

rolled oats (quick-cooking or old-fashioned)

sugar: light brown, dark brown, confectioners', demerara, granulated white

vanilla bean

SEASONINGS AND MIXES

bouillon: beef granules, chicken cubes

bread crumbs: dried, panko

broth and stock: beef, chicken, College Inn White Wine & Herb Culinary Broth, mushroom

Kitchen Bouquet

pepper: black (cracked, ground, whole peppercorns); red (crushed flakes, cayenne); white

red curry paste (Thai)

salt: kosher or coarse, seasoned, table

sauce mixes (McCormick Thick & Zesty Tomato Sauce)

soup mix (Lipton's onion)

spices: advieh, allspice (ground, whole), Badia or Goya sazón spice mix, basil, bay leaves, cardamom, chili powder, chipotle chile powder, Chinese five-spice powder, cinnamon (ground, sticks), cloves (ground, whole), coriander (ground, leaves), cumin (ground, seeds), curry powder (mild Sharwood's or Madras), dry mustard (hot, regular), fennel seeds, Fox Point Seasoning (Penzeys), garlic powder, ginger (ground, crystallized), Greek seasoning (Penzeys), Italian seasoning (Penzeys), lemon-herb seasoning, lemon-pepper seasoning, marjoram, mint, mustard seed, nutmeg, onion (powder, minced dried), orange peel (grated), oregano, paprika (red, Hungarian), red chilies (dried), saffron, sage, seasoned spice rub, sesame seeds (white), thyme, tarragon, turmeric

MISCELLANEOUS

coconut (sweetened, flaked)

couscous (pearl or Israeli)

crackers (oyster)

croutons (seasoned)

dried beans and peas: green lentils, black-eyed peas, green split peas, yellow split peas, black beans, navy beans, Great Northern beans

dried fruits: apricots, currants, dark and golden raisins, pitted prunes

dried mushrooms: chanterelles, porcini

juices: apple, pineapple, pomegranate, tomato

liquor: Amaretto, beer (ale, lager), brandy, Grand Marnier, peach schnapps, rum (Myers's dark)

Nilla Wafers

pasta: elbow macaroni, no-cook flat lasagna noodles, manicotti shells, penne rigate, pennette, pipette or miniature shells, wide egg noodles, ziti

peanuts (dry-roasted unsalted)

peanut butter: chunky, creamy

rice: basmati, jasmine

sun-dried tomatoes: julienne-cut

tortillas: 10-inch flour; 6-inch corn

Tostitos Scoops chips

wine: red (burgundy, table); white (chardonnay, table); marsala; sherry (cream, dry)

CANNED GOODS

artichoke hearts (plain)

beans: black, butter, chickpeas, Great Northern, pinto, Bush's chili beans, Bush's mixed beans

chilies (mild green)

clams: chopped, whole

Coco Lopez Cream of Coconut

cranberry sauce (whole berry)

evaporated milk

mandarin orange segments

olives (sliced ripe)

soup: Campbell's Golden Mushroom, Campbell's Cream of Chicken with Herbs

tomato paste: plain; with basil, garlic, and oregano

tomato sauce: plain; with basil, garlic, and oregano

tomatoes (diced): with basil, garlic, and oregano; with green chilies; Hunt's Diced Fire Roasted Tomatoes with Garlic; Ro-Tel Diced Tomatoes & Green Chilies

tomatoes (petite-diced): plain; in garlic and olive oil

tomatoes (whole): San Marzano peeled plum or Roma

tomatoes (crushed or pureed): plain; with herbs

V-8 juice

JARRED OR BOTTLED GOODS

Asian sweet chili sauce

barbecue sauce (Open Pit Original Flavor)

Bennetts Chili Sauce

black bean dip

brown bean sauce

Busha Browne's Spicy & Hot Pepper Sherry

capers

clam juice

cocktail sauce

fish sauce

grape leaves

honey

hot sauce: Tabasco, Louisiana, Frank's Red Hot Buffalo

hoisin sauce

jams/jellies/marmalades: apricot preserves, orange marmalade, red currant jelly

ketchup

mint sauce

molasses

mustard: Dijon, fruit-flavored honey mustard

oils: olive, canola, vegetable oil spray, toasted sesame

olives: Greek black pitted, pimento-stuffed green, green pitted without pimento, kalamata

ponzu sauce

roasted red peppers

salad dressing: Catalina, ranch

salsa: thick and chunky medium spiced, tomatillo medium spiced

soy sauce

syrup: maple, tamarind

teriyaki sauce

vinegars: cider, red wine, rice, white balsamic, white wine

Worcestershire sauce

Freezer

BREADS
breads and rolls: white, stale sourdough, French baguette, Kaiser rolls

STAPLE INGREDIENTS
bread crumbs (fresh)

butter

cheese (shredded, crumbled): Four Cheese Mexican, mild and sharp cheddar, mozzarella, plain feta, Monterey Jack

citrus zest: orange, lemon (see Slow Cooking Tips section)

fruits: unsweetened coconut, sliced peaches, strawberries, Stouffer's Harvest Apples

herbs: basil, chives, cilantro, dill, mint, parsley (curly and flat-leaf), rosemary, sage, thyme (see Slow Cooking Tips section)

juices: (fresh) lemon, lime, orange; (concentrates) orange (see Slow Cooking Tips section)

nuts: almonds (sliced, slivered), pecans, pine nuts (see Slow Cooking Tips section)

vegetables: gold-and-white corn; country-style hash brown shredded potatoes; pearl onions

MEAT, SEAFOOD, AND POULTRY
beef: chuck and lean ground, sirloin steak, boneless beef chuck roast (corn- and grass-fed), beef stew meat, sirloin tip

roast, skirt steak, rump roast, eye of round roast, New York strip steak, beef short ribs, beef brisket, corned beef brisket

bison (ground)

chicken: skinless, boneless breasts; skinless, boneless thighs; cut-up, bone-in pieces; whole roasting

clams (flash-frozen)

lamb: boneless leg, ground, shanks

pork: bone-in chops, boneless loin roast, tenderloins, baby back ribs, country-style ribs, bone-in hickory-smoked ham, ham bone

sausage: (pork) sweet links, mild and spicy bulk, bratwurst; (turkey) Roasted Garlic and Gruyère Cheese; (chicken) Mozzarella and Roasted Garlic; smoked

shrimp (uncooked, shell on): 16/20s

turkey: Butterball boneless turkey breast roast

veal: ground, stew meat

Refrigerator

PRODUCE

apples: Granny Smith, sweet tart

bell peppers: green, orange, red, yellow

berries: blueberries, cranberries, strawberries

carrots: baby, whole

celery

chile peppers: jalapeño, serrano

citrus: oranges, lemons, limes

eggplants (graffiti)

fennel

gingerroot

juices (orange)

kale

leafy greens (baby spinach)

leeks

mushrooms (fresh): baby bella, shiitake, white button

peaches

pineapple

rhubarb

scallions

sweet onions, like Vidalia

Yukon Gold potatoes (These potatoes have a higher sugar content than other potatoes. Store them in a paper bag or perforated plastic bag in crisper drawer of refrigerator.)

DAIRY

butter: salted, unsalted

cheese (chunk): Swiss, Gruyère, Velvetta

cheese (sliced): Swiss

cream cheese (plain)

eggs (large)

heavy whipping cream

margarine

Parmesan cheese (grated)

ricotta cheese

sour cream

yogurt (plain)

MEAT, SEAFOOD, AND POULTRY

bacon (center-cut)

cold cuts: ham, prosciutto, pancetta, salt pork, sopressata, slim chorizo sticks

fish: halibut, snapper, or grouper

rotisserie chicken

seafood: bay scallops, conch, crabmeat (jumbo lump)

MISCELLANEOUS

Gourmet Garden Blends herb pastes (garlic, gingerroot); Gourmet Garden Fresh Blends ethnic herb & spice pastes (Mediterranean, Mexican, Thai)

guacamole

horseradish (prepared)

sauerkraut

EQUIPMENT AND SUPPLIES

- **Slow cookers:** 1½-quart, 2-quart, 4-quart, 5-quart, and 6-quart.

- **Small appliances:** Some recipes call for a blender, food mill, food processor, electric mixer, or gas grill.

- **Pans:** Nonstick skillets and saucepans (small, medium, large), baking sheets.

- **Cooking oil pump sprayer:** Misto is a popular brand found at most stores that sell kitchen supplies. Light olive oil or canola oil works best in the sprayer. Using real cooking oil is more economical, allows for a more even, controllable spray, and is free of the chemicals commonly found in commercial aerosol cooking sprays.

- **Measuring cups:** You need one set of measuring cups for liquids (1-cup, 2-cup, and/or 4-cup glass or plastic calibrated in ounces) and one set for measuring dry ingredients (1 cup, ½ cup, ⅓ cup, ¼ cup).

- **Microplane grater:** One of a cook's best investments is an ultra-sharp microplane grater, available at most stores that sell kitchenware (about $15). You can grate lemon, lime, or orange peel in mere seconds. You can finely grate gingerroot, garlic, onion, or even chocolate.

Slow Cooker Do's and Don'ts

DO defrost foods before cooking so that they reach a safe temperature quickly.

DON'T delay start time or cook frozen items. Bacteria will form.

DO switch temperature to warm setting when food is cooked to hold it for up to two hours.

DON'T hold food on "off" setting for more than one hour after cooking.

DO tip the lid away from the food when removing it, so the condensation liquid under lid doesn't go into slow cooker.

DON'T lift the lid during cooking time to see how things are progressing. Each time you do, it will take the slow cooker 20 to 30 minutes to get back to temperature, thereby increasing cooking time. (When recipes in this book indicate lifting the lid, increased cooking time is already computed.)

DO layer ingredients as directed in recipe.

DON'T stir ingredients during cooking unless recipe calls for it.

DO load slow cooker with ingredients before turning on heat.

DON'T preheat an empty slow cooker insert.

DO reheat already cooked food on stove before transferring to slow cooker to keep hot on "low" or "warm" setting.

DON'T reheat cold cooked food in slow cooker on any setting.

DO use a hot pad when transferring insert or lifting lid. It will be hot.

DON'T wash slow cooker insert until it comes to room temperature.

DO place slow cooker on an uncluttered countertop.

DON'T use an extension cord to plug in slow cooker. Power cord is made intentionally short to minimize danger from tangling, tripping, or dumping over the hot contents of slow cooker.

DO transfer cooked food to a covered container before refrigerating.

DON'T refrigerate cooked food in slow cooker; the insert may crack.

Slow Cooking Tips

- Liquids do not evaporate in a slow cooker. When converting recipes for use in a slow cooker, use half the liquid called for in the original recipe. The condensation under the lid adds ½ to 1 cup liquid during the cooking process.

- If you double a recipe in this book, use twice as many ingredients but only 50 percent more liquid. Make sure you use a slow cooker that is half to two-thirds full when all the ingredients are added. Cooking time will remain the same.

- Use fresh vegetables. Canned or frozen vegetables will overcook. Put tender vegetables, like asparagus or snow peas, into the slow cooker during the final hour of cooking. Root vegetables cook more slowly than meat, so put them in the bottom of the slow cooker and around sides of the meat so they are closer to the heating element walls of the slow cooker. Make sure they are cut in uniform pieces.

- Ground beef should be browned in a skillet on the stove and drained in a colander before placing in the slow cooker so that excess grease is eliminated.

- Cooked pasta doesn't hold up well in the slow cooking process. Pasta is best added to a slow cooker recipe uncooked. When making lasagna or macaroni and cheese, the uncooked pasta forms the backbone of the dish and is placed in the slow cooker at the very start. (Make sure you have plenty of liquid.) For a soup, add the uncooked pasta during the final 30 to 45 minutes of the cooking process.

- Dairy products break down in the slow cooker, so evaporated milk should be used instead of milk or cream when converting recipes to a slow cooker. You can, however, add milk or cream to "finish" the recipe, adding it only in the final 15 minutes of cooking. Use processed cheese instead of regular cheese unless you add the cheese in the final few minutes of cooking.

- Seafood doesn't take long to cook. Add it within the final 30–60 minutes of cooking.

- Stews and casseroles can be held on warm for up to two hours, but dishes with fragile ingredients, such as seafood, dairy products, or pasta, should not be held.

- Figure two hours on "low" heat setting equals one hour on "high" setting, if you want to cook recipes faster.

- Slow cookers are round or oval. Features range from simple "high," "low," and "warm" settings to totally programmable cookers with temperature probes and "shift to warm" settings.

- A well-stocked spice stash is a must, especially when creating ethnic cuisine from around the world. I buy my spices from www.penzeys.com, which sells an exceptionally wide range of fresh spices in small quantities at reasonable prices. Penzeys has retail stores in only a handful of cities in the U.S., but offers a complete color catalog as well as a great website for ordering through the Internet.

- Fresh herbs are used extensively to flavor the unique cuisines of world countries. I buy bundles of fresh herbs when they are inexpensive and plentiful in the summer season: curly and flat-leaf parsley, basil, rosemary, cilantro, chives, thyme, oregano, mint, dill, and sage. I turn on the television, grab a pair of kitchen scissors, and snip the herbs (rinsed and spun-dry) into a bowl as I watch the news or a movie. Then I transfer the herbs to individual zipper bags, label, and freeze them. Frozen herbs will keep in the freezer for a year, are easy to measure, and add a jolt of flavor freshness that dried herbs simply can't muster. (If you do use dried herbs, use one-third to one-half the amount of fresh herbs called for in the recipe, depending upon the age of the dried herbs. Dried herbs lose their potency over time.)

- Another time-saving, flavor-boosting ingredient is herb paste. Gourmet Garden brand finely ground herb pastes (available in the produce section of your supermarket) last for months in the refrigerator and eliminate prep time mincing, chopping, and snipping. I always keep garlic and gingerroot pastes in my refrigerator, but the company also makes red chili pepper, cilantro, basil, and lemongrass pastes as well as three ethnic herb and spice blends — Mediterranean, Thai, and Mexican. Cost is about 19 cents a tablespoon. Check online at www.gourmetgarden.com/us/ to find a retail source near you.

- Countries in the Middle East and the Med Rim use lots of dried fruits and chopped nuts in their traditional dishes. While dried fruits can be kept almost indefinitely in the pantry, only a few roasted nuts, like peanuts and cashews, should be stored this way. I keep bags of chopped walnuts, pecans, macadamia nuts, pistachios, pine nuts, and sliced almonds in my freezer so they don't become rancid. If you are using them in a recipe, you can use them frozen. (If you'd like to sprinkle them atop salads or cooked food as a garnish, dry-toast them first.)

- Fresh citrus juices and grated peel are essential elements in the cuisine of many of the countries surrounding the Mediterranean Sea, where copious amounts of citrus fruits are grown. My supermarket — and probably yours too — sells bags of "overripe" oranges, limes, and lemons for a fraction of the price usually charged for these expensive fruits. If the peel is still unblemished, I grate the citrus with a microplaner *(see Equipment and Supplies list)* and then freeze it in a labeled zipper bag. The juice is always still good, so I squeeze the citrus and freeze the juice in small plastic containers. I also keep small bottles of lemon juice and lime juice in the refrigerator at all times. If a recipe calls for a tablespoon of fresh lemon juice, it is at my fingertips.

* Many recipes call for just a tablespoon of tomato paste or a quarter cup of tomato sauce or even a small amount of pesto. I wrap the unused portion of tomato paste in plastic wrap, forming a cigar-shaped roll, and freeze it. When I need another tablespoon of paste, I simply unroll the plastic wrap and cut off what I need with a sharp paring knife. I freeze extra tomato sauce and pesto in an ice cube tray and store the cubes in labeled zipper bags. I store unused chicken, beef, and vegetable broth in ½-cup plastic containers in the freezer. They defrost in the microwave in seconds.

* I like to use sweet onions, like Vidalia or Walla Walla, in all my recipes. These mild, sweet-tasting onions contain more sugar than the stronger-flavored Spanish yellow onions. Because of the higher sugar content, buy only the amount you'd use within two weeks' time and keep them refrigerated. Shallots, a distant cousin of the onion, store well for months in the refrigerator. Very important in most cuisines of the world, shallots have a mild flavor with a hint of garlic. If a recipe calls for shallots and you don't have them, use an equal amount of chopped onions and add a finely minced clove of garlic.

Some of the conversions in these lists have been slightly rounded for measuring convenience.

VOLUME:

U.S.	metric
¼ teaspoon	1.25 milliliters
½ teaspoon	2.5 milliliters
¾ teaspoon	3.75 milliliters
1 teaspoon	5 milliliters
1 tablespoon (3 teaspoons)	15 milliliters
2 tablespoons	30 milliliters
3 tablespoons	45 milliliters
1 fluid ounce (2 tablespoons)	30 milliliters
¼ cup (4 tablespoons)	60 milliliters
⅓ cup	80 milliliters
½ cup	120 milliliters
⅔ cup	160 milliliters
1 cup	240 milliliters
2 cups (1 pint)	480 milliliters
4 cups (1 quart or 32 ounces)	960 milliliters
1 gallon (4 quarts)	3.8 liters

OVEN TEMPERATURE:

fahrenheit	celsius
250	120
275	140
300	150
325	160
350	180
375	190
400	200
425	220
450	230
475	240
500	260

WEIGHT:

U.S.	metric
1 ounce (by weight)	28 grams
1 pound	448 grams
2.2 pounds	1 kilogram

LENGTH:

U.S.	metric
⅛ inch	3 millimeters
¼ inch	6 millimeters
½ inch	12 millimeters
1 inch	2.5 centimeters

INDEX

150

Acknowledgments

Some things never change: "I get by with a little help from my friends!" My loyal taste-testers are an elite, dedicated group. Many thanks to my long-suffering, never-complaining husband Bob, who really would have preferred a thick, grilled steak after about the 75th slow-cooked test but hung in there with me until the 105th recipe met my satisfaction. And my gratitude again goes to my willing-to-try-anything friends — Vivienne and Frank Afshari, Bill and Sue Hendrick, Ola Lilley, Randy and Susie Williams, and our couples duplicate-bridge group. Your input was invaluable.

And to those folks who augmented the scores of recipes I developed by sharing some of their personal treasures: Linda McGaan, Barbara Geesey, Karrie Hendrick, Bill Hendrick, Suzanne Tobey, Matthew Shearer, Dana Munn, Kim Huffman, Carol Mann, Joan Dougherty, and Frank Afshari — thank you, thank you, thank you!

My gratitude to Sue Haase at Hamilton Beach Brands, Inc. for supplying me with such a great variety of wonderful slow cookers.

To the person who keeps me in the kitchen and has made this cookbook series possible, Megan Hiller at Sellers Publishing Company, thanks for believing in me once again. I so enjoy working with you.

And of course, along with my hubby, thanks to my family: the Rochester Shearers — Brian, Lisa, Bethany, Bobby, and Leia; the Raleigh Wingenbachs — Kristen, John, Ashleigh, Nicholas, and Christopher; and the Florida golden girls — mother June Harbort and aunt Fern Miller. Always hungry and game to try anything, you all helped make this book possible.